★ piece 'n' play ★ quilts

by Judy Martin

CROSLEY-GRIFFITH
PUBLISHING COMPANY, INC.
Grinnell, Iowa

Acknowledgments

Thanks to Jean Nolte for machine quilting. Thanks to Steve Bennett, Chris Hulin, Linda Medhus, Mary Schuchmann, and Jean Nolte for proofreading. Thanks to BenDavid Grabinski for computer assistance. Thanks to Randy, Danny and Amanda for making the photos look good in print. Thanks to Hobbs Bonded Fibers for providing batting. Thanks to Fasco and Moda for supplying some of the fabrics.

ISBN 0-929589-09-2
Published by Crosley-Griffith
Publishing Company, Inc.
P.O. Box 512
Grinnell, IA 50112
(641) 236-4854
toll free in U.S. (800) 642-5615
e-mail: info@judymartin.com
web site: www.judymartin.com

Photography by Brian Birlauf
Birlauf & Steen Photography
Denver, Colorado

Printed in U.S.A. by
Acme Printing
Des Moines, Iowa

Contents

Spring Valley Log Cabin Quilt in a Traditional Straight Furrows Set

"Piece 'n' Play" is a term that I made up to describe the process that has been used to make Log Cabin quilts all along. However, Piece 'n' Play is not just for Log Cabins. It applies equally well to Drunkard's Paths, Rail Fences, and other asymmetrical blocks. Any block that looks different when you turn it different ways is a candidate for Piece 'n' Play. The idea is to follow a pattern to cut and sew the blocks. Then, before stitching blocks together, play with their arrangement.

Although the Piece 'n' Play process is as easy as child's play, the resulting quilts aren't necessarily for kids. They can be as juvenile or as sophisticated as your fabric choices make them.

Creativity with Security

Piece 'n' Play is fun; it's creative; and anyone can master it. Changing the setting won't affect pattern directions; it simply changes the look. Best of all, Piece 'n' Play is risk free. If you don't like what you come up with, you can always assemble your quilt just the way I did for the quilt in the photograph.

You will love the way Piece 'n' Play takes the guesswork out of creating. You get to see exactly what your quilt will look like before deciding on a setting. If you come up with something you don't like, you won't need a seam ripper to fix it. You can simply pick up the blocks and place them some other way. There is no yardage to figure. You change only the way the blocks are turned, so a wide variety of quilts can be made from exactly the same blocks.

Usually, the creative part of making a quilt is front loaded. That is, you make most of the design decisions early in the process. You choose a pattern and fabrics at the start. If you really like the creative part, the middle stages of sewing can drag. With Piece 'n' Play, you can get a lift from the creativity involved in choosing a set. Furthermore, these creative decisions profoundly affect the look of your quilt. The quilt that results from your block play can surprise and delight you in the same way a mystery quilt can. However, with Piece 'n' Play you can choose fabrics with a clear idea of the block in mind.

Simple Piecing

Any asymmetrical block "plays" to some degree. However, the patterns with the most potential for play are the simple ones that form secondary patterns when they interact with their neighbors. For example, easy Log Cabin blocks offer more play possibilities than more complicated basket blocks. This is because the Log Cabins interact to form bands of light and dark across the quilt's surface, whereas the basket blocks simply look upside down or backward when they are turned.

Thunderstruck Quilt in a Traditional Barnraising Set

Riverbed Quilt in a Traditional Sunshine and Shadows Set

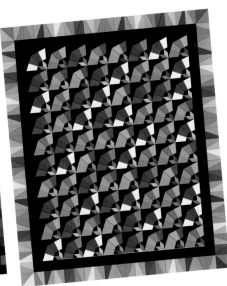

Japanese Fan Quilt in a Traditional Set of Repeating Blocks

■ 3

As a consequence, Piece 'n' Play blocks tend to be exceptionally easy to sew. The quilts in this book are true to form, having blocks consisting of as few as three patches. Half of the quilts have 10 or fewer patches per block.

Dozens of Play Possibilities

With such easy blocks, you will spend less time piecing and more time playing! To get you in a playful frame of mind, I present several arrangements for each pattern. All of the arrangements for a pattern use the same number of blocks as the quilt in the photograph. Use my ideas, or go off on your own. A quick perusal of the book will indicate just how different your quilt can look without altering the yardage, cutting, or block piecing one iota.

Traditional or Contemporary Looks

Arrangements vary from regular, rhythmic traditional arrangements to offbeat, asymmetrical new ones. You are free to go any direction you desire in arranging your blocks.

Innovative, New Designs

All of the blocks in this book are original designs. Ten are my own; one was designed by my son, Will, when he was 10; and one was designed by my husband, Steve, when he was considerably older than 10. All were designed with playing in mind.

Make it a Social Event

Block play is fun, and another opinion is always welcome. Therefore, Piece 'n' Play is perfect for social situations. Invite a friend over when you are ready to play with your blocks. Better yet, convince your friend to make a Piece 'n' Play quilt, too, and you can get together to play when both of you have finished your blocks. If you think more is merrier, have a setting party and invite all your friends.

Piece 'n' Play quilts are also great for classes and challenges. Not only can you get ideas and feedback from others, but also you can all come away from the same class or challenge with strikingly different quilts. You can have a play party to look forward to, as well as a grand finale where the completed quilts are revealed.

Where to Play

Ideally, you should have room to spread out your blocks to play. This can be on a design wall or on the floor. Small quits can be laid out on a bed. If you use a wall, cover it with flannel or some other material to which your blocks will adhere. If you play on the floor, you may want to first lay down a sheet. That way, you'll not only keep your blocks clean, but also you will be able to pin blocks in place and pick your blocks up in a hurry if you need to clear the floor.

If you lack a suitable space, perhaps you can play at a friend's house. Sometimes libraries or churches have meeting rooms that can be reserved for such purposes, as well.

If there is simply no way for you to spread out your blocks to play, you can plan your quilt on paper. This approach has the disadvantage that you can't place individual blocks and rearrange them for color balance, however.

Another Way to Have Fun with Piece 'n' Play

With Piece 'n' Play you can make distinctive, coordinated quilts for a pair of twin beds. Use the same fabrics and block patterns, but change the arrangement to suit the recipient. You can even let the

Roundabout Quilt in a Set that Requires Even Numbers

America, the Beautiful Quilt in a Set Suitable for Odd Numbers

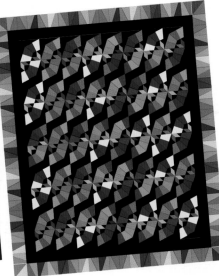

Japanese Fan Quilt in a Set Requiring Even Numbers in Length

recipient participate in arranging the blocks. Make it a special, shared experience, and the quilt will be even more memorable.

Play Basics

Piece 'n' Play blocks have light edges as well as dark edges. You can turn most blocks any of four ways: with the light corner in the upper left, upper right, lower left, or lower right position. If you turn blocks so that matching sides touch in neighboring blocks, you will start to see secondary patterns emerge. These patterns constitute bands of color or value that can be straight or that can turn corners. Light and dark areas can also be arranged to form stars, pinwheels, or other motifs.

After you have arranged your blocks on the wall or floor, look at the overall effect through a reducing glass. Many quilt shops carry a plastic sheet that can either let you view multiple copies of an image or see one image reduced in size. You may be able to accomplish the same thing with your camera lens. You can also stand back from the quilt and squint your eyes (or take off your glasses) to see the secondary pattern emerge.

Standard Traditional Sets

Traditional Log Cabin sets, such as Straight Furrows, Sunshine and Shadows, Barnraising, and others, illustrate some of the more basic possibilities. Because of their familiarity, they are predictable. This quality can strengthen or detract from the feeling you are trying to convey, so be sure to consider whether a regular, traditional look is what you want. Asymmetrical, off-center or otherwise unexpected arrangements make completely different statements. Your choice of sets should take into account your

personal style, the quilt pattern, and the fabrics used in the quilt.

Odd or Even?

Some arrangements require an even number of blocks per row to be symmetrical. For a traditional look, choose Straight Furrows or repeating blocks all in the same orientation if you have an odd number of blocks per row or an odd number of rows. For a more contemporary look, you can choose to arrange your blocks off center or in an irregular setting.

For a traditional look with an even number of blocks per row and an even number of rows, you are free to choose any of the traditional sets, including Barnraising, Sunshine and Shadows, Streak of Lightning, or Straight Furrows. You can also choose an asymmetrical or irregular arrangement for your quilt, if desired.

Mix and Match

Many of the arrangements will work equally well with other blocks from the book, so you can mix and match ideas. Use your imagination, or use the illustrated examples as a guide. At other times, you can adapt a part of a set for use in a different quilt. Some quilts have smaller blocks. Consequently, they have more blocks. Such a quilt might repeat the arrangement of another quilt four times, once in each corner. Conversely, a quilt with larger blocks might be set like a small portion of another quilt.

More Set Ideas

You can also mix two or more set ideas in the same quilt. You can make a medallion of multiple sets. You can start with one set, then reverse the colors for another area. You can also plan one quarter

Riverbed Quilt in a Traditional Straight Furrows Set

Japanese Fan Quilt in a Traditional Straight Furrows Set

Star Shadows Quilt in a Traditional Straight Furrows Set

of the quilt, then repeat it, turning each quarter a different direction.

Mixed Blocks

Several of the quilts in this book are made from two types of blocks in the quilt center. Steve's Star has star blocks and two-triangle blocks. The Midnight Special has Rail Fence blocks and 9-Patch blocks. Family Farm and Roundabout have blocks as well as their reverses in value (lightness or darkness). America, the Beautiful has blocks with white stripes on the outside edge and blocks with red stripes on the outside. In all cases, my quilts use the block pairs in roughly equal quantities. You can simply alternate block types within your chosen set, or you can use the block differences to affect the secondary pattern. Having more kinds of blocks means having more play possibilities!

On Your Own

All of these ideas are simply starting points. Of course, you are free to go any direction your imagination takes you. Feel free to be as rhythmic and repetitive or as free-wheeling as you desire. Have fun with your block play!

Recording Sets

Taking a photograph is a good way to compare different sets to determine which one you prefer. It is far easier to go back and forth between two photos than it is to lay out the blocks over and over again. In this case, instant results are in order. Use a Polaroid or a digital camera for this purpose.

If you have any kind of camera, you can easily preserve setting ideas for use in future quilts. If you have no immediate plans for the set, (or are at the end of a roll of film), you can simply take a snapshot.

If you don't have access to a camera or can't wait for film to develop, you can make one or more photocopies of the quilt from the book. Cut up the copy into blocks. Play with arrangements on paper, and use a glue stick to affix your favorite set(s) onto plain paper. This is also a good way to plan sets before you make blocks, if that is your preference. If photocopying is inconvenient, you can scan the quilt picture into your computer and print it. If you are so equipped, you might scan the block or draw it in your computer. Then you can use a graphics program to turn blocks to make and view different arrangements. If all of these ideas are impractical, you can always resort to paper and pencil.

Shorthand for Planning or Recording Sets on Paper

Sketching your ideas on paper is good whether you just want to idly doodle, you want to quickly record a spontaneous idea, or you have no other way of recording arrangements. For setting purposes, you need not include every detail of the block. The simplest form that shows the secondary pattern will do. For example, many of the quilts in this book have blocks that are split diagonally into light and dark halves. To represent these, I simply divide a square into two triangles and shade one of them. With this shorthand, I can sketch a whole quilt in just a few minutes. Graph paper will make the job simpler as well as neater. It is not necessary to sketch the borders, as they will not change from the pattern.

Another way to record setting ideas is to jot notes in the margins of your book. Suppose you are perusing the book, and you see a setting variation for Riverbed, and you think it would be great for Spring Valley Log Cabin. Make a notation while the idea is fresh. Then, later, when you are ready to make the quilt, you'll remember what you had in mind.

The Long & Winding Road Quilt in an Original Set

Japanese Fan Quilt in an Adaptation of the Same Set

Spring Valley Log Cabin Quilt in an Adaptation of the Same Set

Once you have chosen a favorite layout, you will want to be careful to keep each block in the proper orientation when you join blocks into rows and join the rows to make the quilt. Otherwise, all of your play will have been for naught! You can always leave blocks on the design wall until you are ready to stitch them. However, you can't always leave them on the floor and expect everybody, including the family pets, to ignore them. Anyway, you might get more exercise than you are prepared for if you have to keep going back to the design wall after each seam. Some people simply make their design area portable by covering it with flannel or a sheet that can be removed and carried to the sewing table. You may want to pin blocks to keep them in place.

I can't be bothered to keep referring to the layout and to getting my bearings again. Instead, I label blocks and stack them by rows. I am very consistent in the way I do this so I don't confuse myself any more than usual. When the quilt blocks are arranged as desired on the wall or floor, I make a label for the lefthand block of each horizontal row. The label simply indicates the row number: 1, 2, 3, and so on. I use small scraps of paper and pin a label to the upper lefthand corner of the first block of each row. Sometimes, I use self-adhesive price stickers or folder labels if they are handy. If you use these, make sure to stick them in place securely. (Be advised not to leave an adhesive label on the fabric for very long, as it might leave residue.) For subsequent blocks in a row, I put pins in the upper left corner. I plan to join the blocks two by two, so I label them as follows: Every even-numbered block is marked with one pin in the upper left corner. The odd-numbered blocks

(except the first, which is already labeled) are marked with two pins, three pins, and so on consecutively. If you have small blocks and lots of them in a row, this can get to be a lot of pins! In that case, I would go up to about four pins, then change to pins inserted sideways and start with one pin again. If you do anything tricky, write your system on the paper label of the first block to make sure you remember what you meant. Mark each subsequent row the same way, making sure that the paper label on the first block of the row says the row number.

When each block is marked, pick up the blocks as follows: Put the first block on top, then put the second block beneath it, and the third beneath that, and so on. Make a separate stack for each row. The paper or adhesive label listing the row number will be on top of each row.

When joining blocks, deal with one row at a time. Make sure the pin or label is in the upper left corner when you place the blocks side by side as they will appear in the finished quilt. Turn them face to face, noting which side you need to stitch. Pin and stitch. Proceed with the second pair of blocks in the row. Leave the label or pin in the lefthand (odd-numbered) block of each pairing. You can remove the pin in the righthand block. After making block pairs for the first row, join pairs, referring to the number of pins to keep them in order. Continue until the row is completed. Remove all pin markers, leaving the label on the first block of the row. Make all rows in this fashion. Before joining rows, lay them out in order and compare them to your photo or sketch to make sure there are no mistakes. Join rows in order, referring to the labels.

America, the Beautiful Quilt in a New Set for Mixed Blocks

Steve's Star Quilt in a New Set for Mixed Blocks

The Midnight Special Quilt in a New Set for Mixed Blocks

Once you try Piece 'n' Play, you are going to love the creative satisfaction it gives you. You'll want every project to be as rewarding. This book provides 12 complete patterns and innumerable arrangements to keep you busy for quite some time. However, if you find yourself hungering for more Piece 'n' Play patterns, you will find several in my previous books. In some cases, you will be on your own or will need to refer to *Piece 'n' Play Quilts* for setting variations. Among the suitable patterns are the four shown on this page.

My book, *Star Happy Quilts,* has a Piece 'n' Play theme with a twist. Blocks are not split into light and dark areas. Instead, the play possibilities derive from the combination of three different star blocks. Complete patterns for the Star Happy quilt in five sizes are included. Many additional setting ideas are illustrated, as well.

You may own some of my older, out-of-print books that have even more Piece 'n' Play quilts. I have been fascinated by the Piece 'n' Play process since I made my first Log Cabin quilt in 1973. I have included some projects that play in most of my books. *Log Cabin Quilts* and *Scraps, Blocks & Quilts,* in particular, are full of patterns that play.

I hope *Piece 'n' Play Quilts* makes you as excited about the possibilities as I am and that it helps you explore your own creativity. Have fun!

(Clockwise from top left) Fall Foliage
Spectacular from *Cookies 'n' Quilts,* Starlight Log Cabin from *Pieced Borders,*
Star Happy from *Star Happy Quilts,* and Wilderness Log Cabin from *The Creative Pattern Book.*

Read This Box if You Read Nothing Else!

Please note that my easy cutting methods may be different from other methods you have used. I use *lengthwise* strips, not crosswise ones. I promptly subcut my rotary-cut strips into patches.

I also trim points to help align patches for stitching. I use my Point Trimmer tool (see page 96) for trimming points on any 45° angles. I trace the templates in the book and tape them to an old rotary ruler to trim points on patches having odd angles.

Several of the quilt patterns call for my Shapemaker 45 tool (S45). Don't substitute another triangle ruler. The rulings listed will not work with other rulers. I sometimes use the S45 to allow me to cut triangles from the same strip I use to cut other shapes. These triangles are cut from a rectangle instead of a square. It is important that you remember not to cut the rectangle in half diagonally. That would change the angle and dimensions. Instead, cut the rectangle in two using the S45 tool to make two triangles, each with one point already pretrimmed.

Some dimensions are expressed with "+" after the number. This notation means that the number is in sixteenths. You can use my Rotaruler 16 (R16) and follow a line, or you can use a regular ruler and find the space halfway between the listed number and the next higher eighth.

All of the quilts in this book use fat quarters. I list the minimum number required. The quilts in the photographs were made using smaller amounts of a larger number of fabrics. Buy more fat quarters if you want a scrappier look. Realize, though, that you will have leftovers for your stash if you do so.

The cutting layouts are for lengthwise strips (parallel to the selvedge). I cut strips from right to left, then I subcut the horizontal strips. If you prefer to cut vertical strips with strokes away from your body, turn the layout diagrams sideways to follow them.

For scrap quilts, sometimes many colors are used in the quilt, but only one appears in the cutting layout. Pay attention to the quilt photograph and the whole quilt diagram to determine what range of colors was used to make the quilts.

Border dimensions include seam allowances. They do *not* include any extra in case of sewing inaccuracies. (Most people err on the side of making their patchwork too small, anyway.) Add a little extra yardage and cut borders a little longer if it makes you feel better. However, be sure to measure your quilt and trim borders to fit.

Patterns include photos, yardage requirements, instructions, full-size paper templates, rotary cutting directions, piecing diagrams, quilting diagrams, full-size quilting motifs, and setting variations.

Quilt Specifications

Each pattern begins with a listing of the quilt size, block size, and the number and type of units required to make the quilt.

Yardage & Patch Quantities

Each color of fabric is listed in the next section, along with the number of patches required of each type and yardage figures or the number of fat quarters required. Border dimensions, lining, binding, and batting information are found here, as well.

I made some of the quilts with a variety of scraps against a background cut from a single fabric. In these instances, I list yardage (instead of fat quarters) for the background. If you prefer to make your background from fat quarters, you can multiply yardage by four to convert it to fat quarters. You may need a little extra this way, but you can always go out and buy another fat quarter. Conversely, if you prefer to use yardage where I used fat quarters, you can convert to yardage simply by dividing the number of fat quarters by four.

When using yardage, first cut out the borders. Then cut down the remaining fabric into the specific lengths listed in the layouts. (In most cases, this would be 18".) Then you can cut the remaining patches as shown in the cutting layouts.

Fabric requirements listed allow for the usual shrinkage. Buy a little extra if you are worried about making cutting errors. (Better yet, use fat quarters and buy an extra one!)

Cutting Layouts

Cutting layouts show strip widths for rotary cutting and show how many and what kinds of patches to cut from a strip. Patches are identified by the same letter in the cutting layouts, full-size templates, diagrams, and instructions. The layouts were carefully planned to maximize the scrappy quality of the quilts by cutting a variety of patches from each fabric. They were also carefully planned to yield the correct number of matched patches. Most of the layouts are for fat quarters.

Details & Patch Cutting

The cutting layouts are followed by diagrams showing how to rotary cut each patch. These diagrams are in alphabetical order, not in the order shown on the cutting layout. A patch is diagrammed only once for a pattern, although it may be cut from several fabric colors. Therefore, the color of the diagram may be different from that in a cutting layout.

Be sure to look over the cutting layouts and diagrams before you begin cutting. Note especially the way I lay the ruler over the angled end of the strip for diamonds and for some of the pointy triangles. A long, wide ruler, such as my Rotaruler 16, (page 96) is useful for some of these shapes.

A Note About Reversed Patches

When a pattern calls for a patch and its mirror image, the mirror image is indicated by the patch letter followed by "r." Cut the reversed patch using the diagram for the patch having the same letter. However, cut the reverse with the fabric face down. In the cutting layouts, the face of the fabric is shown, so reverses appear as the mirror images they will be in the finished quilt.

Sometimes I use a reversed patch that is identical in shape to its mirror image. I do this to reverse the grain in order to keep the straight grain around the edges of the block or unit. In such a case, I usually cut the patch and its reverse both at once by cutting through fabric that has been folded in half.

Block Piecing Diagrams

Colored diagrams with captions show you each step of making the quilt. Each block diagram is labeled with the quantity needed to make the quilt. This makes it easy to find the information you need at a glance. A letter is assigned to each patch type. Blocks are exploded to show the first patches joined into subunits and also to show subunits joined to make larger units or rows. Generally, the first patches to be joined are close together, and the later parts are farther and farther apart in the diagram.

Whole Quilt Diagrams

My quilts often have border blocks and corner blocks in addition to the blocks in the quilt center. The whole quilt diagram will help you keep track of the various blocks and units. I don't usually explode these diagrams because the piecing is straightforward. Occasionally, patches as well as blocks are indicated in the quilt diagram. Block letters are from the end of the alphabet to contrast with patch letters, which are from the beginning of the alphabet.

A Note About Bindings

The term "doubled binding" denotes binding that is two layers thick. It is made by joining strips, then folding and pressing the entire length of binding in half (lengthwise) with right sides out. The two raw edges together are stitched to the front of the quilt; then the binding is wrapped around the quilt's edge, and the fold is hand stitched on the back.

Pattern Templates

There are optional full-sized paper templates for you to trace if you use traditional methods. Seam lines are dashed. Cutting lines are solid. Arrows indicate straight (lengthwise) grain. Some patterns also have quilting motifs indicated with heavy dashed lines. Pink dots are for use in aligning quilting repeats. Points are trimmed for neater, more precise patchwork. In a few instances, patterns would be larger than the page, and I present diagrams and cutting dimensions instead of full-sized patches.

If you prefer, the quilts can be rotary cut following the directions provided. Even if you rotary cut, you may find the paper templates handy as a reference for grain lines, letter designations used in the cutting instructions and piecing diagrams, and point trims. If you like, use the templates to check your rotary cutting accuracy.

Quilting Patterns

Illustrated quilting instructions are provided for each quilt. Some can be marked with masking tape. Others will require you to trace a motif given in the book. Many of the quilting patterns are suitable for machine quilting as well as for hand quilting.

Setting Variations

These are drawings of the same quilt with the blocks turned differently. They use the same yardage and instructions as the pattern quilt. They are presented as suggestions only. Feel free to arrange your blocks any way you see fit. Many of the setting variations can be the basis for arranging other blocks in the book. Mix and match ideas to maximize the play possibilities and to multiply your fun.

Paper Piecing Option for Steve's Star

Steve's Star is made from odd-shaped patches that do not lend themselves to rotary cutting. I give you the option of using templates or paper foundation piecing. (I actually cut out the quilt with paper templates taped to my rotary ruler.)

If you knew me, you would be startled that I would suggest paper piecing. I am not fond of the method myself. However, I realize that many people like the method, and it gives them the confidence to tackle a project that they might otherwise be reluctant to try.

If you use paper piecing, be sure to buy extra yardage—quite a bit extra. Paper piecing is not known for its efficiency. You will need to cut oversized strips or patches and later cut them down.

Paper piecing also makes it difficult to place the straight grain of the fabric on the outside edges of these blocks. If you are paper piecing Steve's Star, it is important to leave the paper foundations attached until you have completed all of the blocks and sewn them together to complete the quilt top.

Star Shadow

Star Shadow is an original design by Judy Martin. It was pieced by Judy and quilted by Jean Nolte in 2002. It features Sawtooth Stars that appear to overlap their shadows. It also has a background that is divided diagonally into light and dark halves. The background shading produces Log Cabin-like effects when you play with the block arrangement.

The rotary cutting is streamlined with the use of the Shapemaker 45 tool from Judy Martin. The quilt is made from fat quarters. Each block is made from four fabrics, and Judy's clever cutting layouts result in just the right numbers of matching patches.

Quilt Size: 80" x 90" twin/double
Block Size: 10"

Set: 6 x 7 blocks
Requires: 42 blocks, S45 tool

Yardage & Patch Quantities & Border, Binding & Lining Dimensions

Dark Prints: 14 fat quarters
(for background) Cut 3 blocks per fat qtr.
84 C, 42 D, 42 E, 42 Er, 60 F.

Light Prints: 18 fat quarters
(for background) Cut 2–3 blocks per fat qtr.
borders (abutted):
  2 strips 3" x 70½" (sides)
  2 strips 3" x 65½" (top/bottom)

84 C, 42 D, 42 E, 42 Er, 56 F.

Bright Prints: 11 fat quarters
(for whole stars) Cut 3–4 blocks per fat qtr.
42 A, 336 B.

Contrasting Prints: 6 fat quarters
(for half stars) Cut 7–8 blocks per fat qtr.
168 B, 84 C, 42 D.

Red Prints: 2½ yds. or 7 fat quarters
borders (abutted):
  4 strips 5½" x 80½" (sides/top/bottom)

Doubled Binding: ¾ yd. or 3 fat quarters
  2" x 10 yards

Lining: 7½ yds. or 30 fat quarters
  3 panels 32" x 84"

Batting: 84" x 94"

At-a-Glance Rotary Cutting Layouts for Each Fabric

Dark Prints

1 block (x 42) 3 each fat qtr.

E   C   C   Er   — 2-1/2"
3"   F   F   D   — 2-1/2"
18" lengthwise grain

Dark Prints
Cut 2 F's from
the first 18 fat
quarters. After
that, cut 1 F
from each.

Contrasting Prints

1 block (x 42) 7 or 8 each fat qtr.

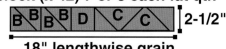
B B B B D   C   C   — 2-1/2"
18" lengthwise grain

Light Prints

1 block (x 18) 1 each fat qtr.

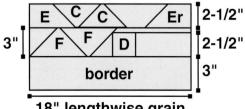
E   C   C   Er   — 2-1/2"
3"   F   F   D   — 2-1/2"
border   — 3"
18" lengthwise grain

1 block (x 24) 1 or 2 each fat qtr.

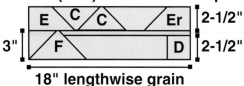
E   C   C   Er   — 2-1/2"
3"   F   D   — 2-1/2"
18" lengthwise grain

Red Border

1 fat quarter (x 7)

border   — 5-1/2"
border   — 5-1/2"
border   — 5-1/2"
18" lengthwise grain

Binding

1 fat quarter (x 3)

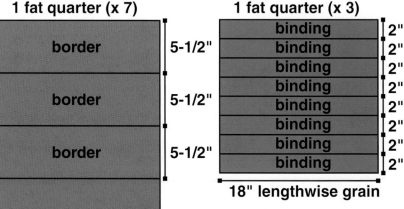
binding — 2"
binding — 2"
binding — 2"
binding — 2"
binding — 2"
binding — 2"
binding — 2"
binding — 2"
18" lengthwise grain

Bright Prints

1 block (x 42) 3 or 4 each fat qtr.

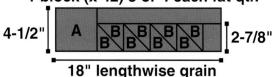
4-1/2"   A   B B B B / B B B B   — 2-7/8"
18" lengthwise grain

Lining

x 3 panels

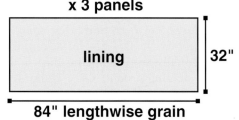
lining   — 32"
84" lengthwise grain

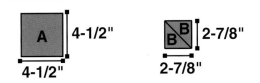

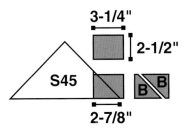

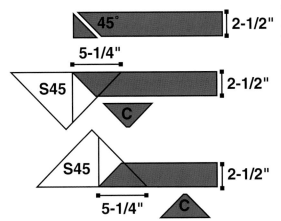

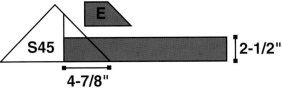

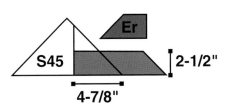

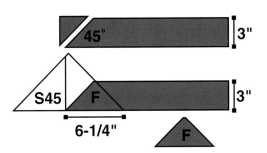

A: Cut strip 4½" x 18". Square up end with clean cut. Subcut square 4½".

Bright B: Cut strip to a width of 2⅞". Subcut squares 2⅞". Cut each square in half along one diagonal to make triangles. Trim points.

Contrasting B: Note that the contrasting B is the same finished patch as the bright print B. However, the contrasting B is cut from the narrower strip needed for the C and D patches. Therefore, this B is cut 2 to a rectangle, and the rectangle is not cut along its diagonal. Instead, it is cut using the S45 tool.

Cut strip 2½" wide. Subcut rectangles 3¼". Subcut each rectangle to make 2 triangles using the Shapemaker 45 tool as follows: Align the 2⅞" line of the S45 tool with short end of rectangle. (The tool's point is about ⅜" from the corner.) Align long edge of S45 even with long side of rectangle. Cut along the angled end of the tool to make two triangles, each with one point pretrimmed. Trim remaining point of each triangle.

C: Cut strip 2½" wide. Cut off end at 45° angle. Lay the S45 tool over the remaining part of strip. Align the pointed end of the strip with the 5¼" line on the tool. Align the long edge of the tool even with the long edge of the strip. Cut along the angled end of the tool to complete triangle. Rotate S45 tool and cut a second triangle next to the first one, as shown. Trim points.

D: Cut strip and square 2½".

E: Cut strip 2½" x 18". Square up ends with clean cuts. Lay the Shapemaker 45 tool over strip, aligning left end of strip with 4⅞" line on ruler and aligning long edge of S45 tool with long side of strip. Cut along the angled edge of tool to complete trapezoid as shown. Trim point.

Er: Turn 2½" strip face down with the square end on the left. Cut as you did for E. Because the fabric is face down, your patch will be a reverse of E. Trim point.

F: Note: Cut 2 F's from each of the first 18 block sets. Thereafter, cut only 1 F per block set. Cut strip 3" x 18". Cut off end at 45° angle. Lay the S45 tool over the remaining part of strip. Align the pointed end of the strip with the 6¼" line on the tool. Align the long edge of the tool even with the long edge of the strip. Cut along the angled end of the tool to complete triangle. Rotate S45 tool and cut a second triangle next to the first one. Trim points.

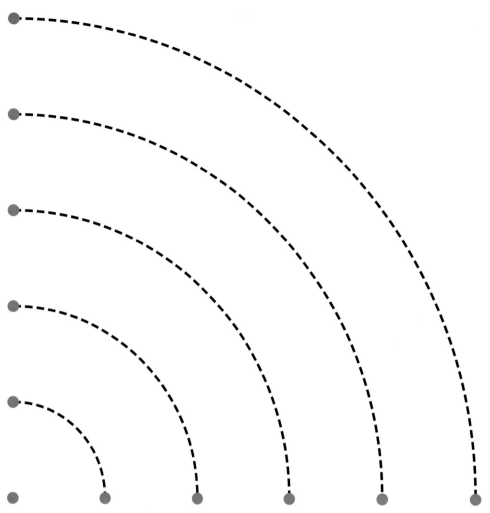

Full-Size Border Quilting
Match dots to complete circles.

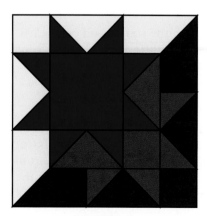

42 X Blocks

**Optional Color
Placement for X Block**

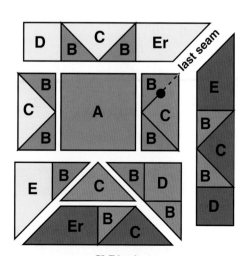

X Piecing
(Dot indicates end of partial seam.)

For the best shadow effect, make the half star darker or less bright than the whole star. Choose scrap combinations to allow the star to contrast with the half star as well as the background. You may place either the dark or the light background next to the whole star, depending on optimal contrasts, as shown in the block diagrams on page 14.

Arrange patches for a block as shown. Sew 1 C triangle in the shadow color to a B triangle in a star color with a partial seam as indicated by the dot in the diagram. That is, sew only halfway down the side of the C patch, starting at the square end of C and ending at the dot. Complete the rest of the block before completing the partial seam. Make 42 blocks.

Arrange blocks in 7 rows of 6 blocks each. Play with turning the blocks to make the secondary pattern of your choice. Join blocks into rows. Join rows.

Join 5 light border strips each for two side borders and 4 light strips each for top and bottom borders. Measure your quilt center and cut the borders to fit. (Ideal sizes are on page 12.) Pin and sew the longer light borders to long sides of quilt. Pin and sew shorter light borders to top and bottom of quilt.

Join 15 light F triangles alternately with 14 dark F's and sew to long side of quilt. Repeat for opposite side. Join 13 light F's alternately with 12 dark F's and sew to top of quilt. Repeat for bottom. Join 2 dark F's and sew to border corner. Repeat for each corner.

Join 5 red border strips for each border. Measure your quilt center and cut the borders to fit. Ideally, they should be cut 5½" x 80½" (all 4 sides). Pin and sew red borders to long sides of quilt. Pin and sew the remaining red borders to the top and bottom.

Whole Quilt Diagram

Mark the motif on page 18 in each whole star. (It is not necessary to mark in the ditch.) Trace the motif from page 14 four times on paper to complete the circles. Mark circles as shown below in borders, centering them on the points of F triangles.

Baste the layers together. Quilt as marked.

Quilt in the ditch around stars and star shadows and along diagonals between light and dark backgrounds. Quilt diagonal lines through the half stars as shown. Quilt vertical stripes 1" apart in dark block backgrounds. Fill in the light backgrounds with small meandering or stippling (not shown).

Bind the edges of the quilt. Sign and date your quilt to finish it.

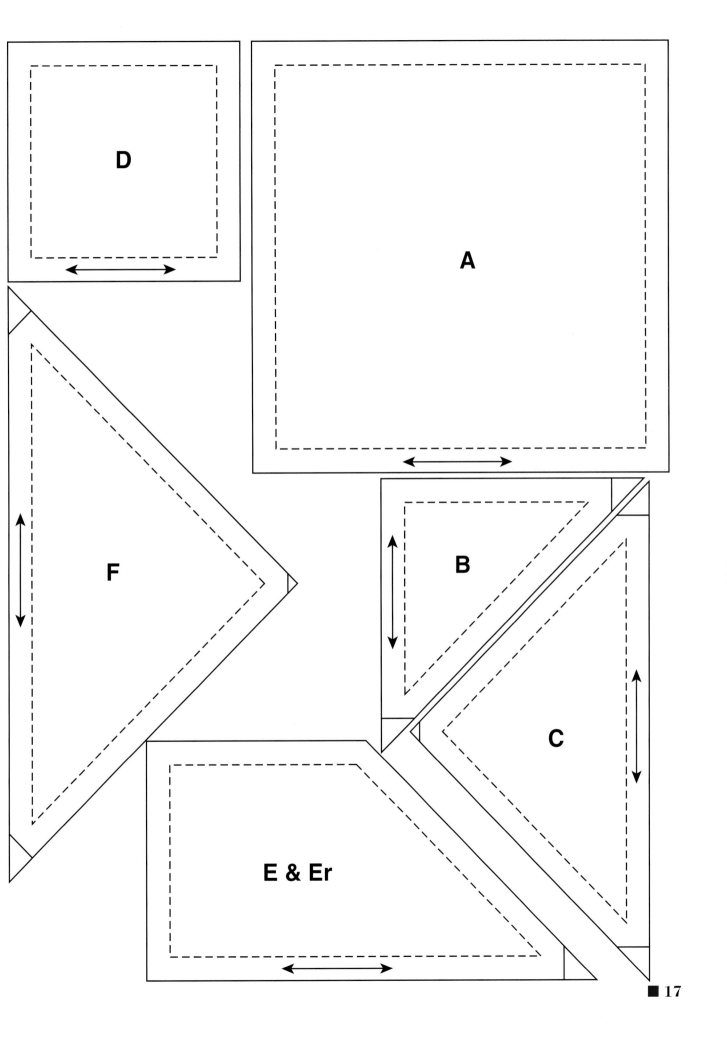

D

A

F

B

C

E & Er

17

Here are four setting variations for the Star Shadow quilt. I have shown these examples in just four colors instead of a scrappy color scheme to enable you to see the secondary patterns more clearly. The star pattern is strong here, so the background division into light and dark halves is more subtle in this quilt than in a Log Cabin, for example.

The top left example features an arrangement I call "Not-So-Straight Furrows." The diagonal bands of color reverse in the center panel to disrupt the straight lines. At the top right is an arrangement of Pinwheels. The Pinwheels, themselves, scarcely show up, but the rhythm is interesting. At the bottom left is a spiral arrangement. It is actually quite similar to a Barnraising. At the bottom right is a pattern of reversing chevrons that make a herringbone-like design. Star Shadow makes a delightful quilt even without the secondary patterns, but the play possibilities are ever so much more fun than the stars alone would be!

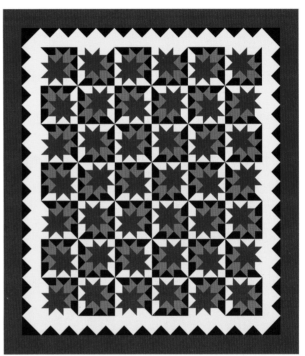

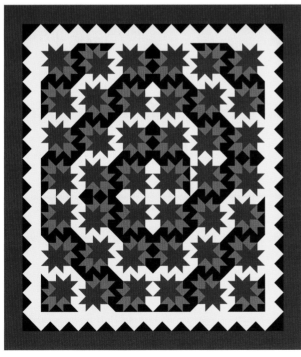

Japanese Fan

Designed and pieced by Judy Martin; quilted by Jean Nolte, 2002. My Japanese Fan was inspired by the traditional block, but I eliminated the curves and appliqué and added the diamonds for a filigreed effect. This is a terrific pattern for showing off those gorgeous Japanese-style fabrics you have been collecting. Their brilliant colors and golden accents are set off beautifully by the black background. The illusion of curves makes Japanese Fan a standout in any arrangement. Batting is gray polyester by Hobbs.

Quilt Size: 72" x 86" twin
Block Sizes: 7" X, 4½" x 7" Y, 4½" Z

Set: 8 x 10 blocks
Requires: 80 X, 40 Y, 4 Z, S45, R16 (optional)

Yardage & Patch Quantities & Border, Binding & Lining Dimensions

Black Print: 3¾ yards
borders (abutted):
  2 strips 4" x 70½" (sides)
  2 strips 4" x 63½" (top/bottom)

160 B, 160 Br, 80 D, 80 Dr.

Bright Prints: 27 fat quarters
160 A, 160 C, 160 Cr, 80 E, 80 Er, 8 F.

Doubled Binding: ¾ yd. or 3 fat quarters
  2" x 9⅛ yards

Lining: 5⅜ yds. or 24 fat quarters
  2 panels 39" x 90"

Batting: 76" x 90"

At-a-Glance Rotary Cutting Layouts for Each Fabric

Black Print

3-3/4 yards black (allows for shrinkage)

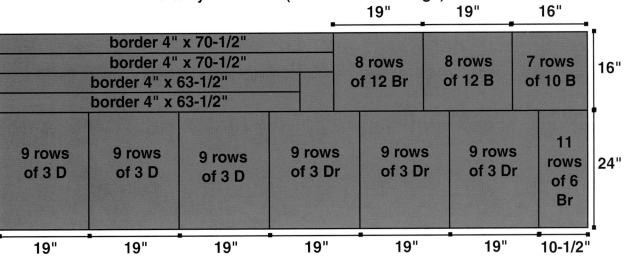

Detail of Black Cutting Layout is on next page.

Bright Prints

Binding

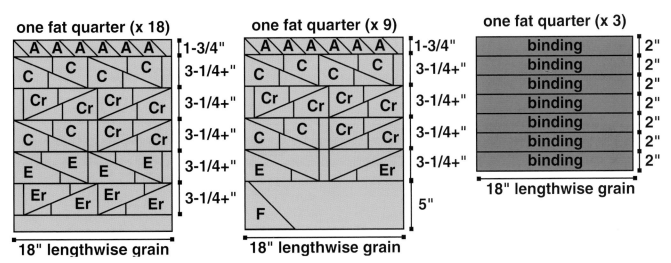

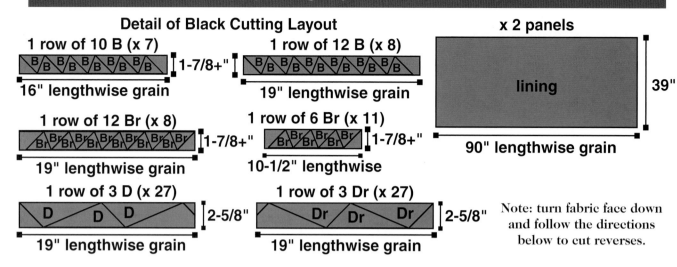

Detail of Black Cutting Layout

1 row of 10 B (x 7) 1-7/8+"
16" lengthwise grain

1 row of 12 B (x 8) 1-7/8+"
19" lengthwise grain

x 2 panels

lining 39"

90" lengthwise grain

1 row of 12 Br (x 8) 1-7/8+"
19" lengthwise grain

1 row of 6 Br (x 11) 1-7/8+"
10-1/2" lengthwise

1 row of 3 D (x 27) 2-5/8"
19" lengthwise grain

1 row of 3 Dr (x 27) 2-5/8"
19" lengthwise grain

Note: turn fabric face down and follow the directions below to cut reverses.

Details & Patch Cutting Dimensions for Cutting Layouts

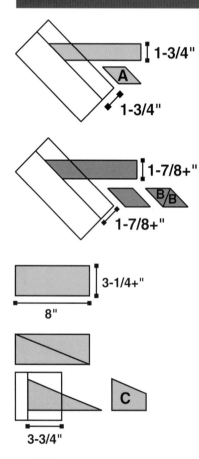

1-3/4"
1-3/4"
A

1-7/8+"
1-7/8+"
B/B

3-1/4+"
8"

3-3/4"
C

A. Cut strip 1¾". Cut off end at 45° angle. Lay 1¾" ruling over angled end, and cut diamond A.

B. Cut strip 1⅞+" (halfway between 1⅞" and 2"). Cut off end at 45° angle. Lay the 1⅞+" ruling over angled end of strip. Cut diamond. Cut in half diagonally to make 2 B's.

C. Cut strip 3¼+" (halfway between 3¼" and 3⅜"). Cut 8" rectangle. Cut in half diagonally to make 2 triangles. Lay 3¾" ruling over short end of triangle and cut off point to make C.

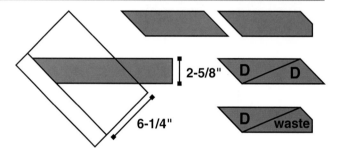

2-5/8" D D
6-1/4"
D waste

D. Cut strip 2⅝". Cut off end at 45° angle. Lay 6¼" ruling over angled end, and make parallel cuts. Cut from corner to corner as shown to make 3 D triangles.

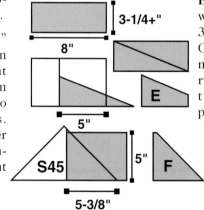

3-1/4+"
8"
5"
E
5"
S45 F
5-3/8"

E. Cut strip 3¼+" (halfway between 3¼" and 3⅜"). Cut 8" rectangle. Cut in half diagonally to make 2 triangles. Lay 5" ruling over short end of triangle and cut off point to make E.

F. Cut 5" strip. Lay 5⅜" ruling of S45 over squared end of strip and cut along angled edge.

Construction

Make 80 X blocks, 40 Y blocks, and 4 Z blocks as shown on page 23.

Arrange X blocks in 10 rows of 8 blocks each. Play with arrangements until you find the one you like best. Join blocks to make rows. Join rows.

Add longer black borders to sides of quilt. Add shorter black borders to top and bottom of quilt.

Join 11 Y blocks for a side border. Sew to side of quilt. Repeat for the opposite side. Join 9 Y blocks for the top of quilt; add a Z to each end, referring to the quilt diagram on the next page. Attach. Repeat for the bottom of the quilt.

To finish the quilt, refer to the quilting directions above the quilting diagram on page 24.

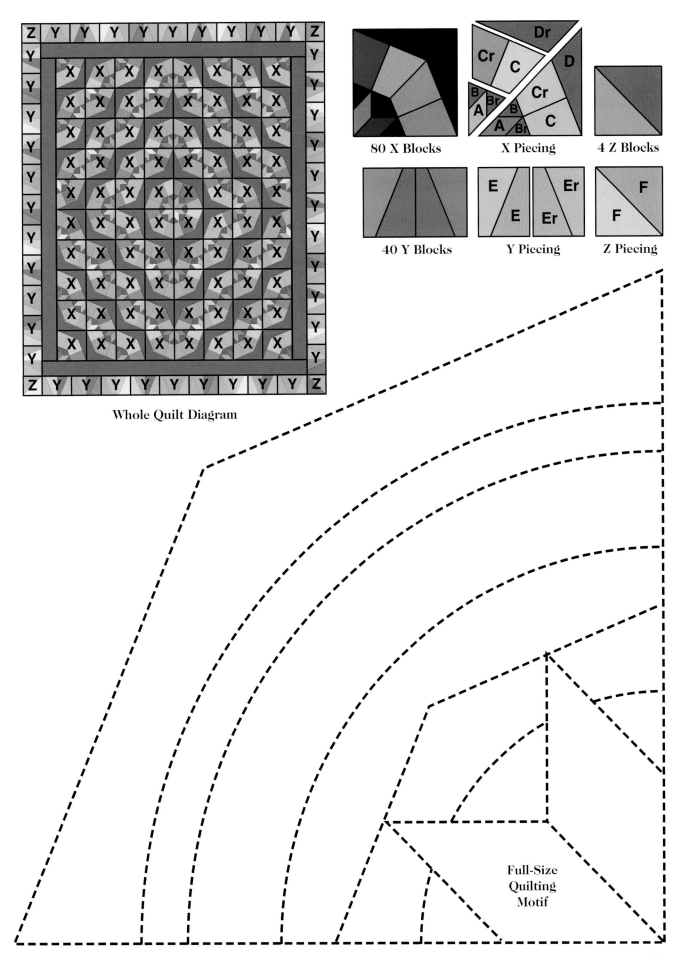

Whole Quilt Diagram

80 X Blocks

X Piecing

4 Z Blocks

40 Y Blocks

Y Piecing

Z Piecing

Full-Size
Quilting
Motif

In each block, mark quarter-circles from the quilting motif on page 23.

Baste the layers together. Quilt as marked.

Quilt in the ditch as indicated in the full-size motif on page 23. Quilt in the ditch along both edges of the black inner border and around E, Er, and F patches of the pieced borders.

Use masking tape to mark diagonal stripes 1" apart in the black background and black border. Begin quilting these stripes in the ditch between the short sides of D and Dr patches, and mark off 1" intervals from there. Change the direction of the stripes at the midlines of the quilt.

Bind the edges. Sign and date to finish your quilt.

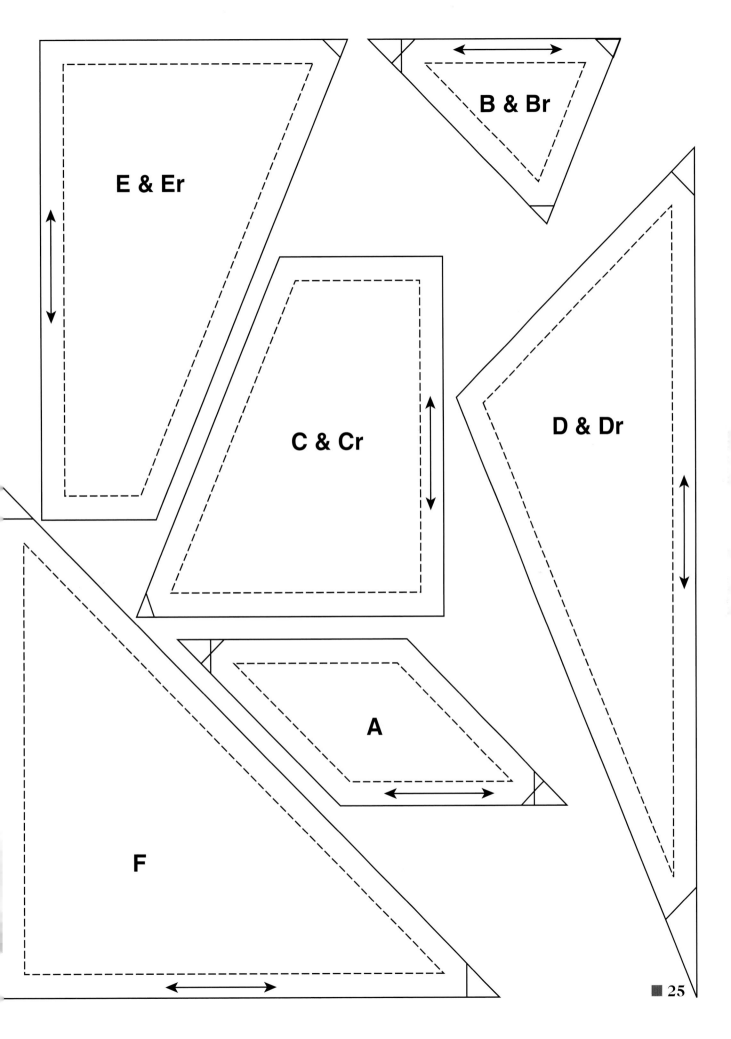

E & Er

B & Br

C & Cr

D & Dr

A

F

■ 25

The Japanese Fan blocks combine to make circles, partial circles, undulating trails, and scallops as shown below. The top left example suggests a 3-dimensional pyramid built of stacked circles. At top right, six circles are framed with a scalloped border.

The two examples at the bottom of the page, as well as the quilt in the photo on page 20, are variations of a Barnraising set. One has a black star in the center, another has a circle surrounded by half circles, and the photo quilt has a simple circle in the center.

Roundabout

Designed and made by Judy Martin, 2002. Roundabout was inspired by the traditional Drunkard's Path. Here, again, I eliminated the curves. I also divided the colored areas into squares to echo a Double Wedding Ring. Simple, straight seams make this quilt a joy to cut and sew. Its blocks in two colorings play in all of the old Drunkard's Path sets and the Log Cabin sets, as well. You will want to allow plenty of play time, because this quilt is exceptionally handsome in a wide variety of arrangements.

Quilt Size: 72" x 90" twin
Block Sizes: 4½" X, 4½" Y, 1½" Z

Set: 12 x 16 blocks
Requires: 96 X, 96 Y, 196 Z, R16 (optional)

Yardage & Patch Quantities & Border, Binding & Lining Dimensions

Cream Print: 4¾ yards
borders (abutted):
   2 strips 5" x 72½" (sides)
   2 strips 5" x 63½" (top/bottom)

192 A, 196 B, 192 C.

Bright Prints: 20 fat quarters
borders (abutted):
   2 strips 3½" x 84½" (sides)

2 strips 3½" x 72½" (top/bottom)

768 A, 388 B.

Doubled Binding: ¾ yd. or 3 fat quarters
   2" x 9½ yards

Lining: 5⅝ yds. or 24 fat quarters
   2 panels 39" x 94"

Batting: 76" x 94"

At-a-Glance Rotary Cutting Layouts for Each Fabric

Cream Print

4-3/4 yards cream (allows for shrinkage)

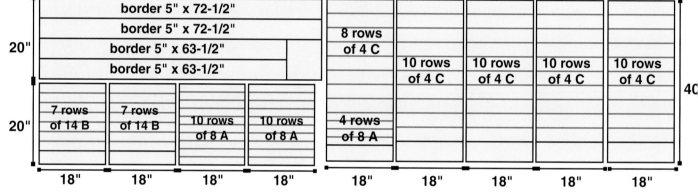

Detail of Cream Layout

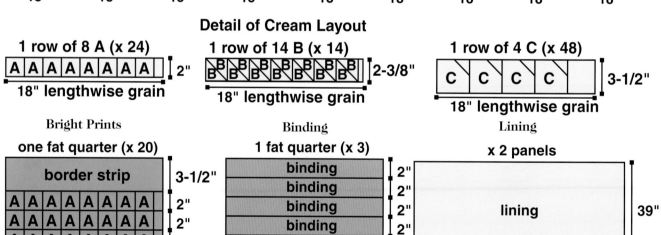

1 row of 8 A (x 24)
18" lengthwise grain

1 row of 14 B (x 14)
18" lengthwise grain

1 row of 4 C (x 48)
18" lengthwise grain

Bright Prints
one fat quarter (x 20)
18" lengthwise grain

Binding
1 fat quarter (x 3)
18" lengthwise grain

Lining
x 2 panels
94" lengthwise grain

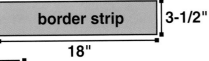

border strip | 3-1/2"
18"

A | 2"
2"

B B | 2-3/8"
2-3/8"

Bright Border. Cut strip 3½" wide x 18" long.

A. Cut 2" strip and square.

B. Cut 2⅜" strip and square. Cut in half along diagonal to make 2 B's.

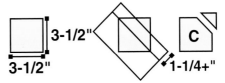

3-1/2"
3-1/2"

C

1-1/4+"

C. Cut 3½" strip and square. Lay 1¼" ruling of R16 ruler (page 96) over two opposite corners of square. Cut off corner at the ruler's edge to make C. (If you don't have an R16, find the space halfway between 1¼" and 1⅜".)

Construction

Make 96 X blocks, 96 Y blocks, and 196 Z units.

Play with block arrangements, placing blocks in 16 rows of 12 blocks each. Join blocks to make rows. Join rows.

Attach the longer cream border strips to the sides of the quilt center. Add shorter cream strips to top and bottom of quilt center.

Join 27 Z units facing the same direction. Join 27 more facing the opposite direction. Join the two segments, with lights touching, to form a side border. Attach to quilt. Repeat for the opposite side.

Similarly join 22 Z facing one way and 22 Z facing the opposite way for the top border. Attach. Repeat for the bottom of the quilt. Add longer bright borders to sides. Add shorter ones to top and bottom.

To finish the quilt, refer to page 31.

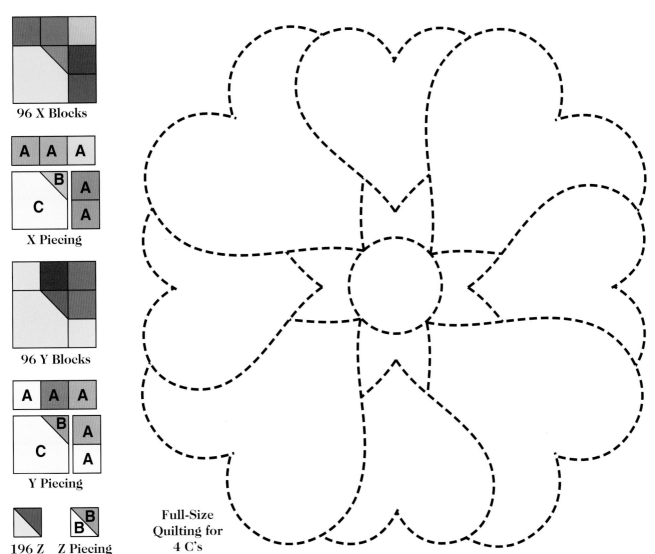

96 X Blocks

| A | A | A |

B
C | A
A

X Piecing

96 Y Blocks

| A | A | A |

B
C | A
A

Y Piecing

196 Z | Z Piecing B B

Full-Size
Quilting for
4 C's

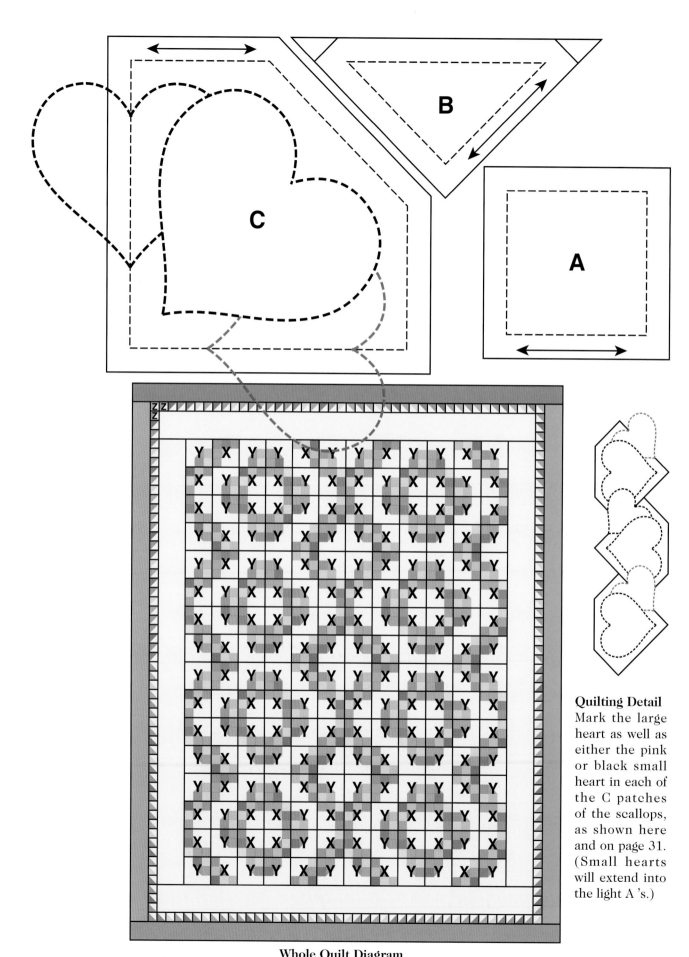

C

B

A

Quilting Detail
Mark the large heart as well as either the pink or black small heart in each of the C patches of the scallops, as shown here and on page 31. (Small hearts will extend into the light A's.)

Whole Quilt Diagram

Quilting

Mark the 8-heart and 2-heart motifs from pages 29 and 30 in C patches and neighboring light squares as shown below.

Baste the layers together. Quilt as marked. Quilt in the ditch around dark squares and triangles in the quilt center and between light and dark triangles of the borders.

Use masking tape to mark and quilt horizontal stripes ¾" apart in the background of the quilt center and light side borders. Similarly quilt ¾" vertical stripes in the top and bottom light borders. Quilt the border corners as shown.

Continue the diagonal lines of quilting from the long sides of the border triangles through the dark outer borders. Quilt the corners as shown.

Bind the edges, sign and date your quilt to finish it.

The light and dark Roundabout blocks can be combined to make circles, flowers, crosses, scallops, undulating bands, and more. Often, as in the top left example, blocks are arranged to make bigger blocks before they are joined into rows. At the top right is an example of blocks organized into vertical chains. At the bottom left is a Barnraising with a change of rhythm in the corners. This is accomplished with a reversal of colors. At the bottom right is an adaptation of four small Barnraisings.

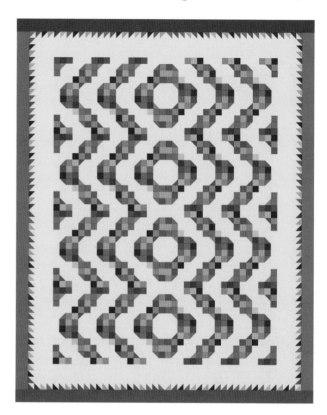

The Long & Winding Road

Designed and pieced by Judy Martin; quilted by Jean Nolte, 2002. The Long & Winding Road was inspired by the traditional Drunkard's Path. I straightened out the curve and split the block to avoid set-in seams. The result is an extremely easy block made from just four patches. The cutting may be new to you, but it is not difficult. Furthermore, the sewing is a cinch! An old-fashioned kite border finishes the quilt with a flourish. It involves several more new shapes, but the look is worth the effort. Batting is 100% organic cotton with scrim from Hobbs Bonded Fibers.

Quilt Size: 76½" x 91½" twin/double
Block Sizes: 3¾" X, 3¾" x 6⅜" Y, 6⅜" Z

Set: 16 x 20 blocks
Requires: 320 X, 76 Y, 4 Z

Yardage & Patch Quantities & Border, Binding & Lining Dimensions

Bright Prints: 27 fat quarters
320 A, 320 Ar, 80 C, 76 Cr, 4 D, 4 F, 4 Fr.

Light Prints: 30 fat quarters
borders (abutted):
 2 strips 2⅜" x 75½" (sides)
 2 strips 2⅜" x 64¼" (top/bottom)

320 B, 320 Br, 80 D, 80 Dr, 156 E, 4 G, 4Gr.

Doubled Binding: ¾ yd. or 3 fat quarters
 2" x 9¾ yards

Lining: 7¼ yds. or 30 fat quarters
 3 panels 33" x 81"

Batting: 81" x 96"

At-a-Glance Rotary Cutting Layouts for Each Fabric

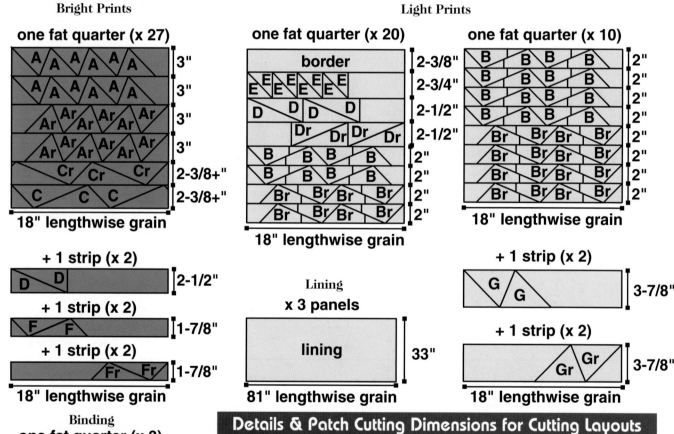

Details & Patch Cutting Dimensions for Cutting Layouts

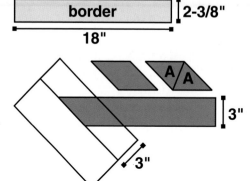

Border. Cut a strip 2⅜" wide x 18" long.

A. Cut 3" strip. Cut off end at a 45° angle. Lay 3" rule line on angled end and cut diamond. Cut diamond in half diagonally to make 2 A triangles.

Note: Cut reverse patches for A, B, C, D, F, and G as shown, except do so with the fabric turned face down.

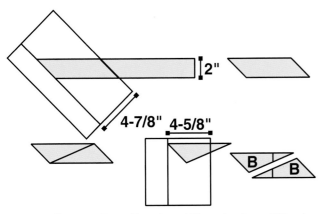

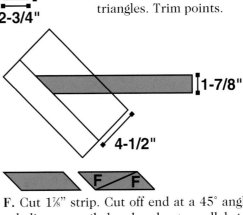

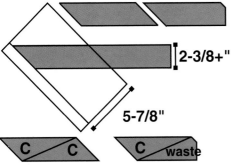

E. Cut 2¾" strip and square. Cut in half along one diagonal to make 2 E triangles. Trim points.

B. Cut 2" strip. Cut off end at 45° angle. Lay 4⅞" rule line on angled end and cut parallelogram. Cut in half diagonally. Align long edge of patch with a rule line and 45° point with 4⅞" ruling. Cut off point for B.

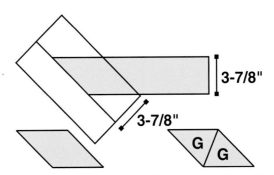

F. Cut 1⅞" strip. Cut off end at a 45° angle. Lay 4½" rule line on angled end and cut parallelogram. Cut in half diagonally to make 2 F triangles.

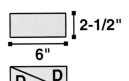

C. Cut 2⅜+" strip. (Use Rotaruler 16, page 96, or cut halfway between 2⅜" and 2½".) Cut off end at a 45° angle. Lay 5⅞" rule line on angled end and make parallel cuts. Cut from corner to corner to make 3 C's.

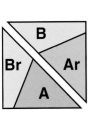

D. Cut 2½" strip. Cut 6" rectangle. Cut in half diagonally to make 2 D triangles.

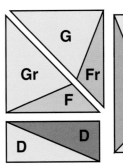

G. Cut 3⅞" strip. Cut off end at a 45° angle. Lay 3⅞" rule line on angled end and cut diamond. Cut diamond in half diagonally to make 2 G triangles.

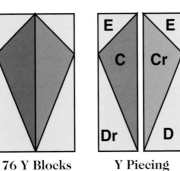

320 X Blocks

76 Y Blocks

Y Piecing

4 Z Blocks

Z Piecing

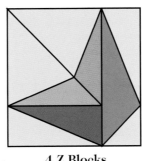

X Piecing

Make 320 X blocks for the quilt center as shown on page 35. Make 76 Y blocks for the borders and 4 Z blocks for the corners. Play with block arrangements, placing X blocks in 20 rows of 16 blocks each. Join blocks to make rows. Join rows.

Attach the longer border strips to the sides of the quilt. Add shorter strips to top and bottom of quilt.

Make pieced borders for long side as follows: Join 21 Y blocks; sew to quilt. Repeat for other side. For top of quilt, join 17 Y blocks; add a Z to each end, turning as shown below; sew to top of quilt. Repeat for bottom.

To finish the quilt, see the quilting directions above the quilting diagram on page 37.

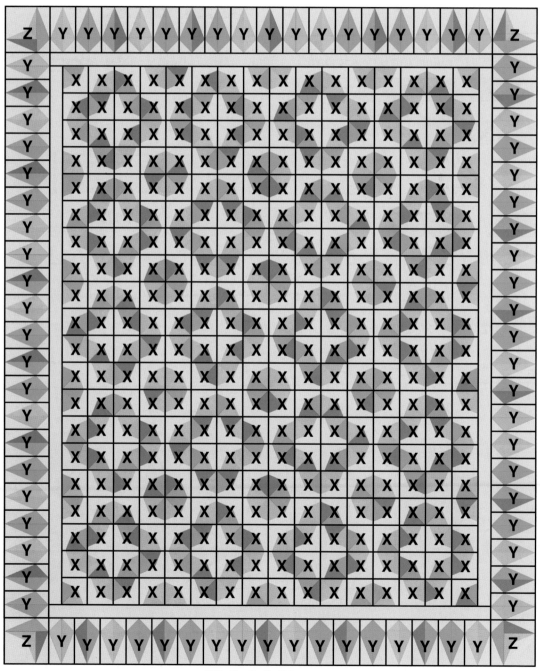

Whole Quilt Diagram

You may want to vary the quilting pattern based on your block arrangement.

Baste the layers together.

Quilt in the ditch around the dark patches. Quilt in the ditch along inner edge of plain border. Use masking tape to mark quilting lines ½" in from dark patches wherever 4 B and 4 Br patches meet. These lines form a four-pointed star. Quilt an "x" in the ditch in the middle of each of these stars.

Quilt parallel lines about ⅞" apart in the remaining light areas of the quilt center, as shown below.

Quilt three parallel lines ⅜" apart in the light areas of the borders to form a zigzag pattern, as shown.

Bind the quilt's edges. Sign and date to finish it.

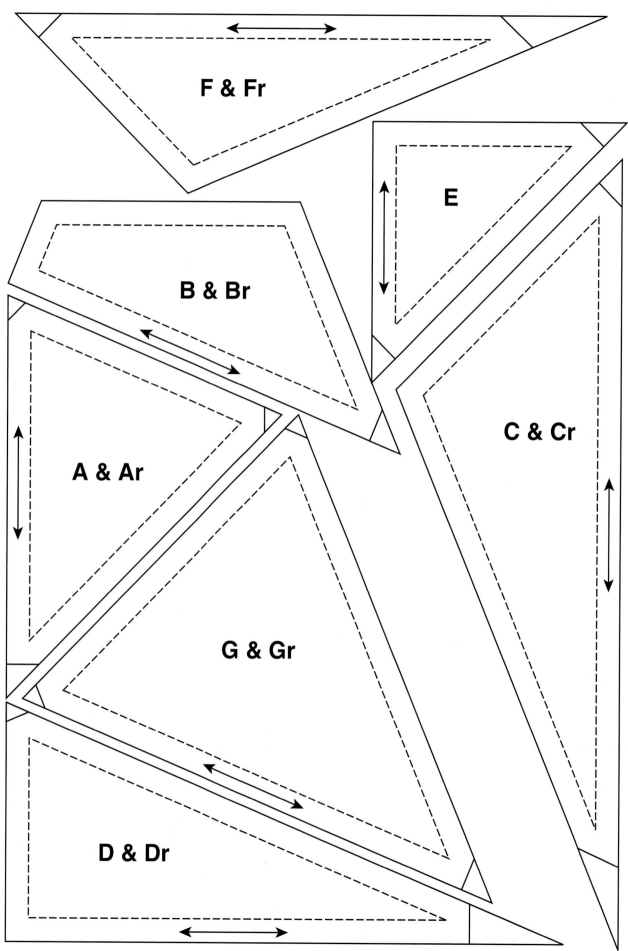

F & Fr

E

B & Br

C & Cr

A & Ar

G & Gr

D & Dr

Circles, partial circles, and undulating bands are just some of the effects you can achieve with The Long & Winding Road. In the top left example, blocks are arranged in sets of 16 to make Grand Blocks that look like rippling water. At the top right is a quilt with blocks forming two ribbon borders around a central medallion. At the bottom left is a Barnraising that is interspersed with circles. At the bottom right is a medallion featuring a pyramid that appears to be made of stacked circles. The blocks surrounding that form a border that resembles Flying Geese. Because the Long & Winding Road block is so small, arrangements can be as complex as you care to imagine.

The Midnight Special

Designed and made by Judy Martin, 2000. Here, Rail Fence blocks alternate with 9-Patch blocks. To suggest a cross superimposed on a Rail Fence, I matched same-colored patches within a block. My cutting layouts result in suitable quantities of matching patches. The staggered 9-Patch border adds a perfect finishing touch. I chose an arrangement that expanded on the usual Rail Fence zigzag. Here, though, the stripes continue through two blocks (a Rail Fence and a 9-Patch) before changing direction. The sewing is extremely easy, and the play adds to the fun quotient. Many of the fabrics are from Moda.

Quilt Size: 70" x 94" twin/double
Block Sizes: 6" V, W; 6" x 8" X, Y; 8" Z

Set: 9 x 13 blocks
Requires: 59 V, 58 W, 24 X, 20 Y, 4 Z

Yardage & Patch Quantities & Binding & Lining Dimensions

Black Prints: 11 fat quarters
218 A, 86 B.

Red Prints: 11 fat quarters
214 A, 82 B.

Cream Prints: 11 fat quarters
428 A.

Pumpkin Prints: 7 fat quarters
107 A, 58 B.

Doubled Binding: ¾ yd. or 3 fat quarters
2" x 9½ yards

Lining: 5⅞ yds. or 24 fat quarters
2 panels 38" x 98"

Batting: 74" x 98"

At-a-Glance Rotary Cutting Layouts for Each Fabric

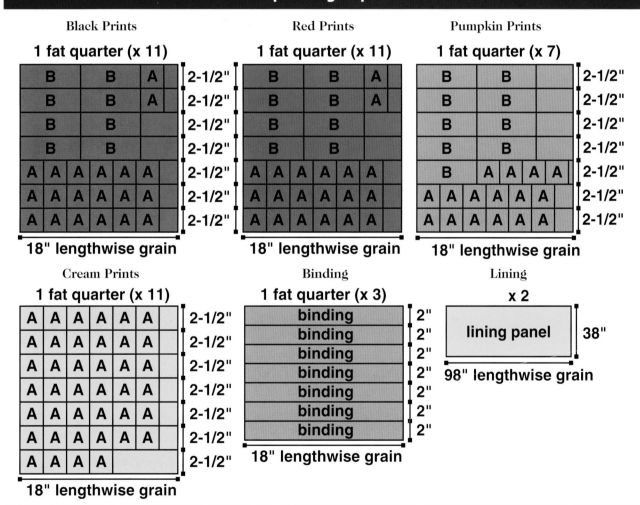

Details & Patch Cutting Dimensions for Cutting Layouts

A. Cut strip and square 2½".

B. Cut strip 2½". Cut rectangle 6½".

■ 41

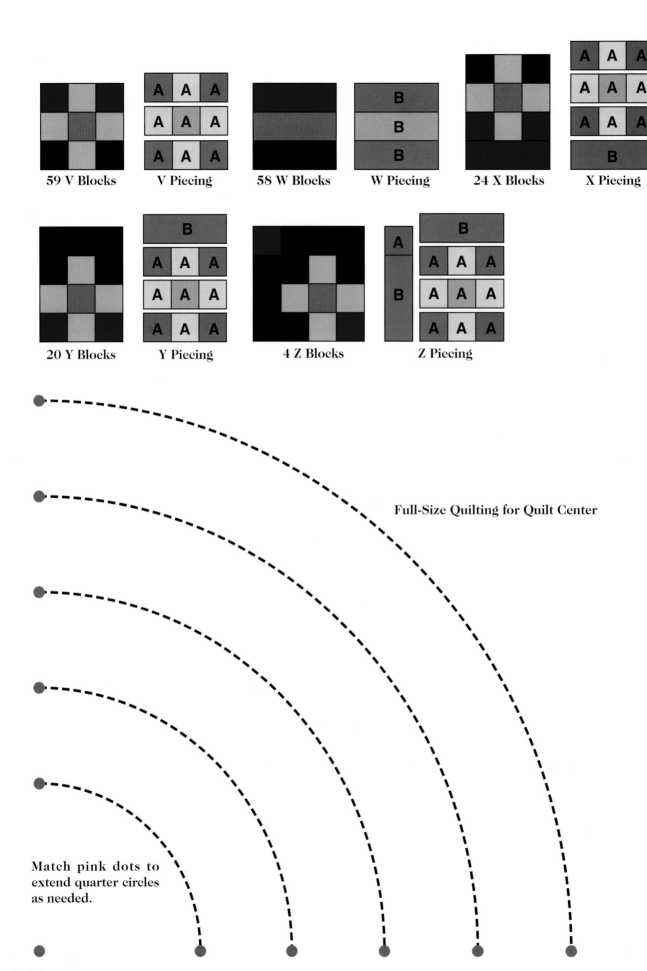

59 V Blocks   V Piecing   58 W Blocks   W Piecing   24 X Blocks   X Piecing

20 Y Blocks   Y Piecing   4 Z Blocks   Z Piecing

Full-Size Quilting for Quilt Center

Match pink dots to
extend quarter circles
as needed.

Make 59 V blocks, 58 W blocks, 24 X blocks, 20 Y blocks, and 4 Z blocks, as shown on page 42.

Arrange V blocks and W blocks in 13 rows of 9 blocks each. Keep playing with the arrangement until you have a favorite. Join blocks to make rows. Join rows to complete the quilt center.

Join 7 X blocks alternately with 6 Y blocks to make a side border, turning units as shown in the quilt diagram below. Sew to side of quilt. Repeat for opposite side. For the top border, join 5 X blocks alternately with 4 Y blocks and add a Z to each end, as shown. Sew to top of quilt. Repeat for the bottom.

To finish the quilt, refer to the quilting directions above the quilting diagram on the next page .

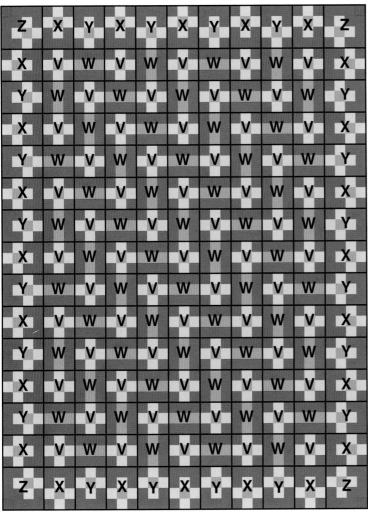

Whole Quilt Diagram

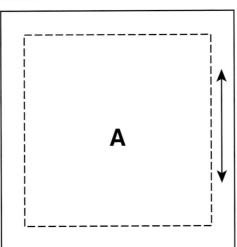

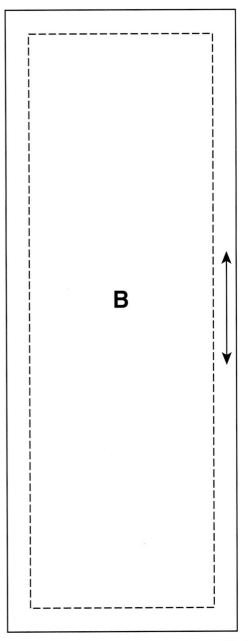

In the quilt center, mark Baptist Fans using the concentric quarter-circles from page 42, and extending them where needed. Start in the lower left corner, and center circles 6" apart in block corners.

Baste the layers together. Quilt as marked.

Quilt in the ditch between the quilt center and the border. Also quilt in the ditch around cream squares in border. Use masking tape to mark stripes 1" apart in the borders as shown. Quilt as marked.

Bind the edges. Sign and date your quilt to finish.

Rail Fence blocks have surprisingly good play possibilities. In the typical Rail Fence, vertical blocks alternate with horizontal ones. However, you can change the look by stringing together two or more blocks in the same direction before turning the corner. Stripes, boxes, zigzags, and L shapes, as well as weaving patterns such as basket weave, satin weave, and herringbone are just a few of the possibilities.

Riverbed

Designed and made by Judy Martin, 2002. When I designed this quilt, I had in mind a Japanese garden. I wanted the colors to reflect earth, stone, sand, and vegetation, with all its varying undertones. I found batiks to have the tonal variation that I desired. The light half of each block is made from parallel logs to suggest raked sand. The dark half is made principally from squares that approximate the rhythm of pebbles. I thought that an asymmetrical arrangement would best suit this contemporary-looking quilt.

Quilt Size: 72" x 90" twin
Block Sizes: 9" X, 6" x 9" Y, 9" Z

Set: 6 x 8 blocks
Requires: 48 X, 42 Y, 4 Z

Light Prints: 16 fat quarters
52 A, 102 B, 136 C, 90 D, 48 E.

Dark Prints: 21 fat quarters
284 A, 98 B, 48 C, 248 F.

Doubled Binding: ¾ yd. or 3 fat quarters
 2" x 9½ yards

Lining: 5½ yds. or 24 fat quarters
 2 panels 39" x 94"

Batting: 76" x 94"

At-a-Glance Rotary Cutting Layouts for Each Fabric

Light Prints

1 fat quarter (x 16)

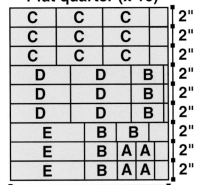

18" lengthwise grain

Dark Prints

1 fat quarter (x 21)

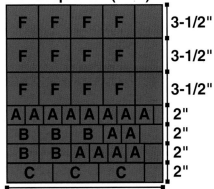

18" lengthwise grain

Binding

1 fat quarter (x 3)

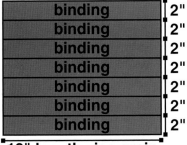

18" lengthwise grain

Lining

x 2 panels

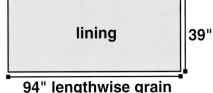

94" lengthwise grain

Details & Patch Cutting Dimensions for Cutting Layouts

A. Cut 2" strip and square.

B. Cut 2" strip. Cut 3½" rectangle.

C. Cut 2" strip. Cut 5" rectangle. Note that you need to cut 3 C's from only the first 6 dark fat quarters. Thereafter, cut 2 C's per fat quarter.

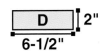
D. Cut 2" strip. Cut 6½" rectangle.

B. Cut 2" strip. Cut 8" rectangle.

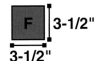
F. Cut 3½" strip and square.

■ 47

Make 48 X blocks, 42 Y blocks, and 4 Z blocks as shown below.

Arrange the X blocks in 8 rows of 6 blocks each. Play with the arrangement until you decide on a favorite. Join blocks to make rows. Join rows.

See the whole quilt diagram on page 49. Join 12 Y blocks to make a side border. Sew to one side of the quilt. Repeat for the opposite side. Join 9 Y blocks; add a Z to each end. Sew to the top of the quilt. Repeat for the bottom.

To finish the quilt, refer to the quilting instructions above the quilting diagram on page 50.

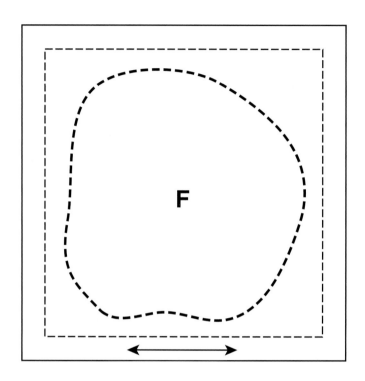

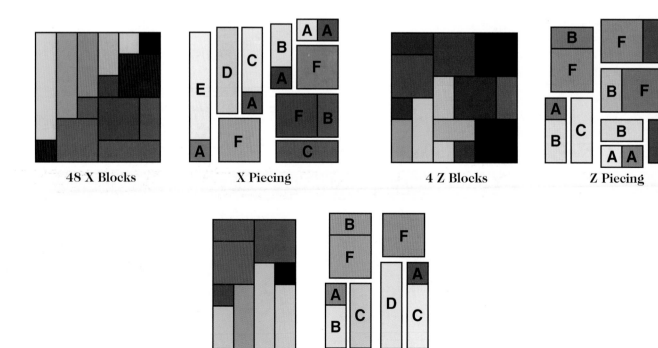

48 X Blocks   X Piecing   4 Z Blocks   Z Piecing

42 Y Blocks   Y Piecing

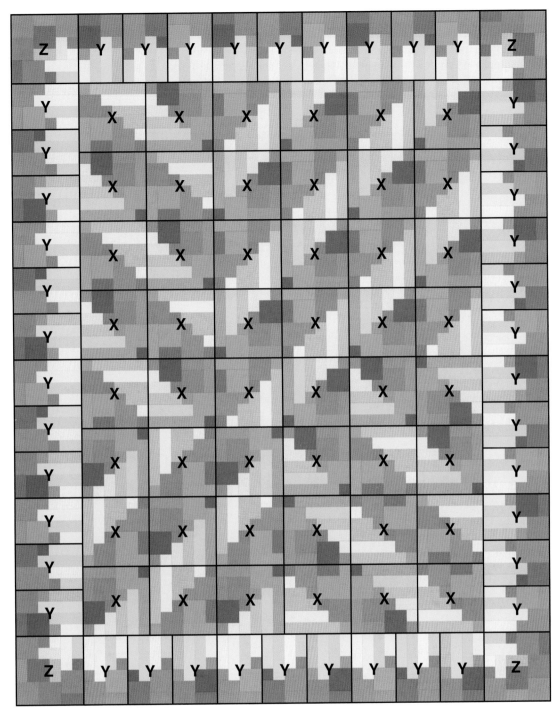

Whole Quilt Diagram

In the dark A, B, C, and F patches, mark the pebble motifs from pages 48 and 51. If desired, stipple the space between pebbles to puff up the pebbles.

Baste the layers together. Quilt as marked.

Quilt in the ditch between light and dark areas.

Use ¾" masking take to mark and quilt stripes down the light log centers, as shown. Quilt in the ditch between light logs. Note the way the stripes turn in the corner units.

Bind the edges. Sign and date the quilt to finish it.

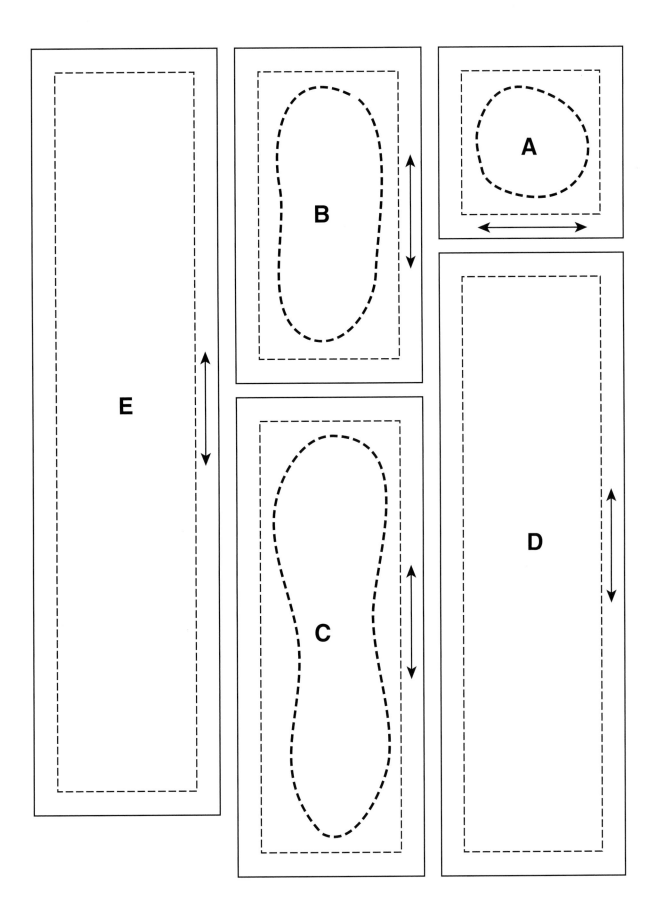

Riverbed plays in all the usual Log Cabin sets and in original arrangements, as well. At top left is a combination of the traditional sets Sunshine and Shadows and Streak of Lightning. Light block edges touch light to form squares, and dark edges touch dark to make zigzags. At top right is a star framed with chevrons and triangles. At the bottom left is a combination of Square in a Square, Birds in Flight, and Barnraising. At the bottom right is a combination of Barnraising and Zigzag elements.

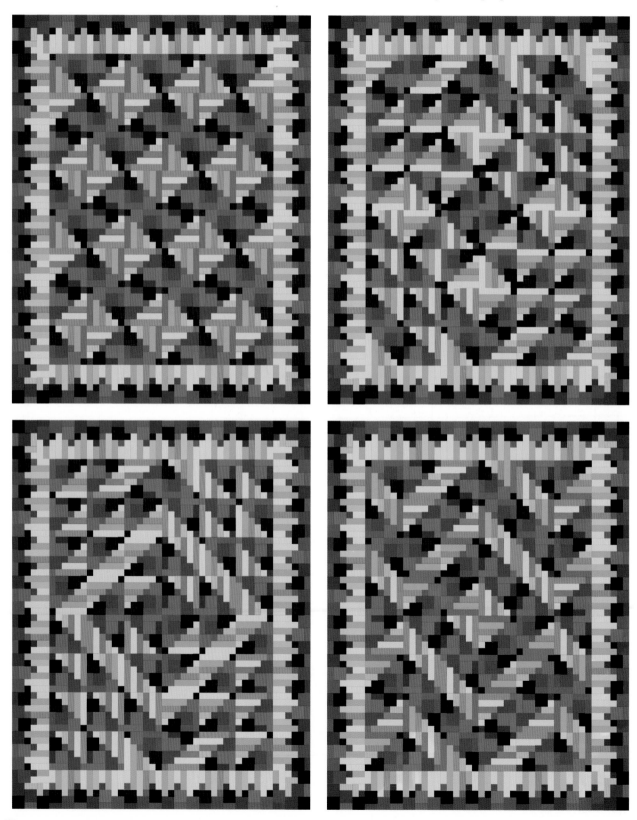

Spring Valley Log Cabin

Designed and pieced by Judy Martin; quilted by Jean Nolte, 2002. Flowers are pieced into a Log Cabin for a jaunty new block that has all the setting possibilities of its forebears. A stair-stepped log border finishes the edges with style. Here, pastel '30s reproduction prints and solids form a soft contrast with a mix of prints having ivory backgrounds. In each block, the two patches that make a flower are cut from the same fabric. Fabrics include pastels from Marcus Brothers and Moda and lights from Marsha McCloskey's Staples by Fasco. Batting is 100% cotton from Hobbs.

Quilt Size: 74" x 94" twin
Block Size: 10" V; 5" x 7" W, X; 7" Y, Z

Set: 6 x 8 blocks
Requires: 48 V, 28 W, 28 X, 2 Y, 2 Z, S45 tool

Yardage & Patch Quantities & Border, Binding & Lining Dimensions

Bright Solids: ½ yd. or 4 fat quarters
(fat quarter qty. includes extra for variety)
48 B, 48 C.
Green Print(s): ½ yd. or 2 fat quarters
96 B, 48 P.

Light Prints: 24 fat quarters
48 A, 96 B, 48 D, 48 Dr, 48 E, 48 Er, 48 F, 48 G, 28 J, 60 Q, 114 R, 84 S.

Bright Prints: 24 fat quarters
48 H, 48 I, 140 J, 172 K, 48 L, 48 M, 48 N, 48 O, 8 Q, 8 R, 36 S, 64 T.

Doubled Binding: ¾ yd. or 3 fat quarters
2" x 9¾ yards

Lining: 5⅞ yds. or 24 fat quarters
2 panels 40" x 98"

Batting: 78" x 98"

At-a-Glance Rotary Cutting Layouts for Each Fabric

Bright Solids

one fat quarter (x 4)

18" lengthwise grain

Light Prints

one fat quarter (x 24)

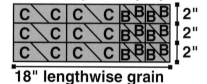

18" lengthwise grain

Light Prints

Cut the second J patch from only the first 4 fat quarters. Thereafter, cut 1 J from each fat quarter.

Binding

one fat quarter (x 3)

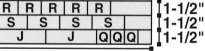

18" lengthwise grain

Green Prints

one fat quarter (x 2)

6 rows of 4 P

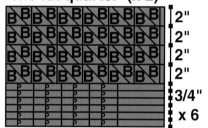

18" lengthwise grain

Bright Prints

one fat quarter (x 24)

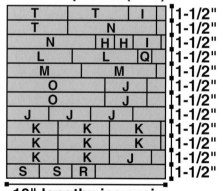

18" lengthwise grain

Lining

x 2 panels

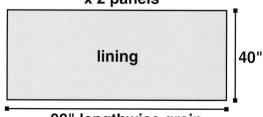

98" lengthwise grain

54

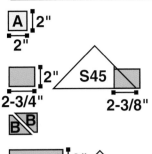

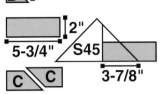

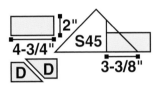

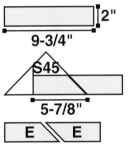

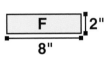

A. Cut 2" strip and square.

B. Cut 2" strip. Cut 2¾" rectangle. Align long edge of S45 tool with long side of rectangle. Align 2⅜" ruling with short side of rectangle. Cut along angled edge to make 2 triangles, each with 1 point already trimmed.

C. Cut 2" strip. Cut 5¾" rectangle. Align long edge of S45 tool with long side of rectangle. Align 3⅞" ruling with short side of rectangle. Cut along angled edge to make 2 C trapezoids.

D. Cut 2" strip. Cut 4¾" rectangle. Align long edge of S45 tool with long side of rectangle. Align 3⅜" ruling with short side of rectangle. Cut along angled edge to make 2 D trapezoids.

E. Cut 2" strip. Cut 9¾" rectangle. Align long edge of S45 tool with long side of rectangle. Align 5⅞" ruling with short side of rectangle. Cut along angled edge to make 2 E trapezoids.

F. Cut 2" strip. Cut 8" rectangle.

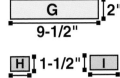

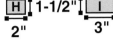

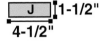

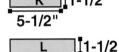

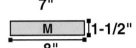

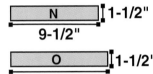

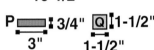

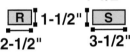

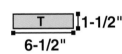

G. Cut 2" strip. Cut 9½" rectangle.

H. Cut 1½" strip. Cut 2" rectangle.

I. Cut 1½" strip. Cut 3" rectangle.

J. Cut 1½" strip. Cut 4½" rectangle.

K. Cut 1½" strip. Cut 5½" rectangle.

L. Cut 1½" strip. Cut 7" rectangle.

M. Cut 1½" strip. Cut 8" rectangle.

N. Cut 1½" strip. Cut 9½" rectangle.

O. Cut 1½" strip. Cut 10½" rectangle.

P. Cut ¾" strip. Cut 3" rectangle.

Q. Cut 1½" strip. Cut 1½" square.

R. Cut 1½" strip. Cut 2½" rectangle.

S. Cut 1½" strip. Cut 3½" rectangle.

T. Cut 1½" strip. Cut 6½" rectangle.

Construction

Referring to the diagrams on page 56 and the stem piecing instructions below, make 48 V blocks for the quilt center. Also make 28 W, 28 X, 2 Y, and 2 Z blocks for the pieced borders. Note that for V, Y, and Z blocks one diagram lists patch letters and another lists piecing sequence. Add patches in numerical order, first joining all patches with the same number to make a "log."

Referring to the quilt photograph and the setting variations on page 60, play with the arrangement of the 48 V blocks. Join blocks to make 8 rows of 6 blocks each. Join rows.

To make the pieced border for the long side, join 8 X blocks alternately with 8 W blocks as shown in the whole quilt diagram on page 56. Sew to the quilt. Repeat for the opposite side. For the top border, join 6 X blocks alternately with 6 W blocks; sew a Z to one end and a Y to the other, as shown. Sew to the top of the quilt. Repeat for the bottom.

Finish the quilt as described on page 57.

Stem Piecing

Fold green P in half lengthwise with right sides out. Press.

Insert the folded P between 2 light B triangles, aligning raw edges. Stitch, press to one side, Trim off stem ends even with B patches.

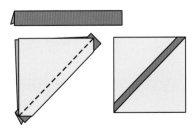

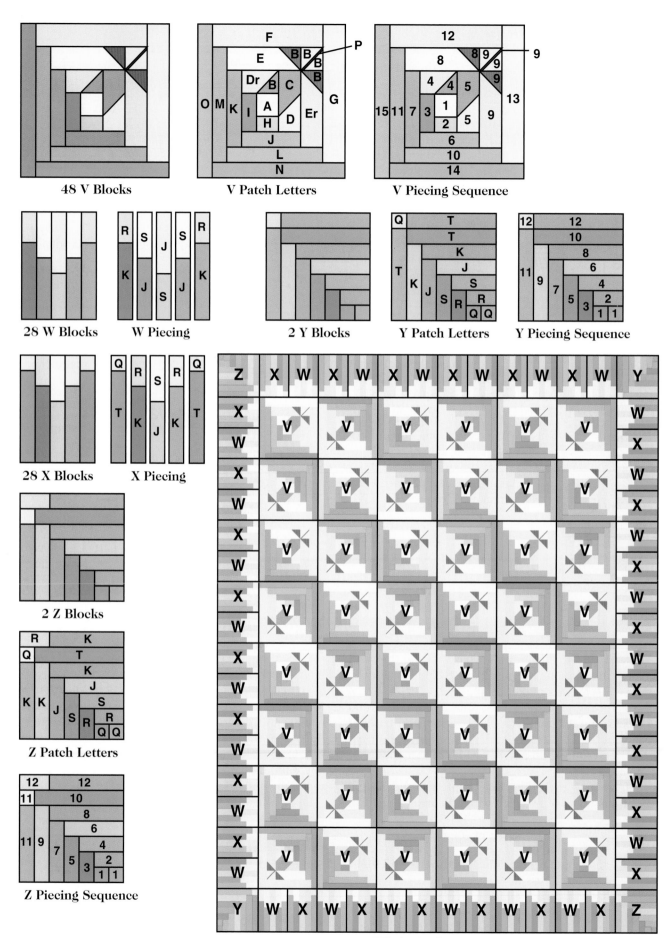

48 V Blocks

V Patch Letters

V Piecing Sequence

28 W Blocks

W Piecing

2 Y Blocks

Y Patch Letters

Y Piecing Sequence

28 X Blocks

X Piecing

2 Z Blocks

Z Patch Letters

Z Piecing Sequence

Whole Quilt Diagram

Make four photocopies of the quarter-circle motif on page 59. Tape them together, matching pink dots, to make a complete circle. Referring to the diagram below, mark the circle motif in the light areas only. The circles should be centered on V block corners as shown, starting with the block in the upper left corner of the quilt. Succeeding circle motifs should not cross the previous ones, but rather start at the outermost part of the circles already marked.

Baste the layers together. Quilt as marked.

Quilt in the ditch around the bright logs, flowers, leaves, and along the stitched edge of each stem.

Attach the binding. Don't forget to sign and date your quilt to finish it.

Note: N and O are shown smaller than their actual sizes, which would be too large for the page.

Also note that patches R, S, J, K, T, L, and M extend to the top of the Q patch.

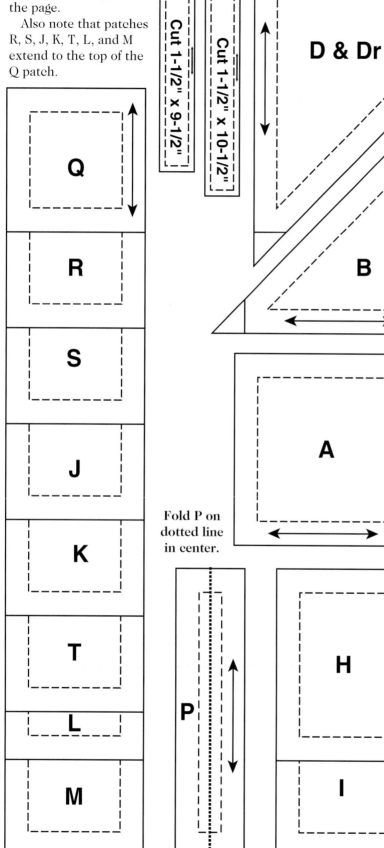

N Cut 1-1/2" x 9-1/2"

O Cut 1-1/2" x 10-1/2"

Q

R

S

J

K

T

L

M

Fold P on dotted line in center.

P

A

D & Dr

B

H

I

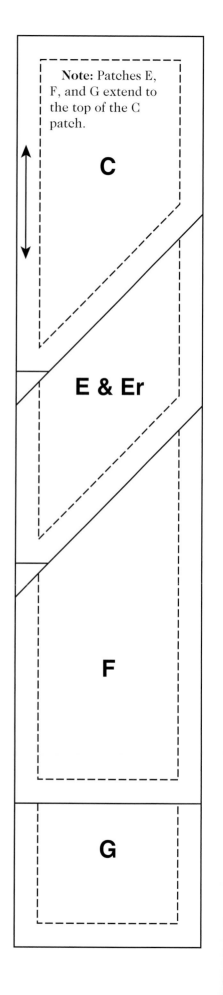

Note: Patches E, F, and G extend to the top of the C patch.

C

E & Er

F

G

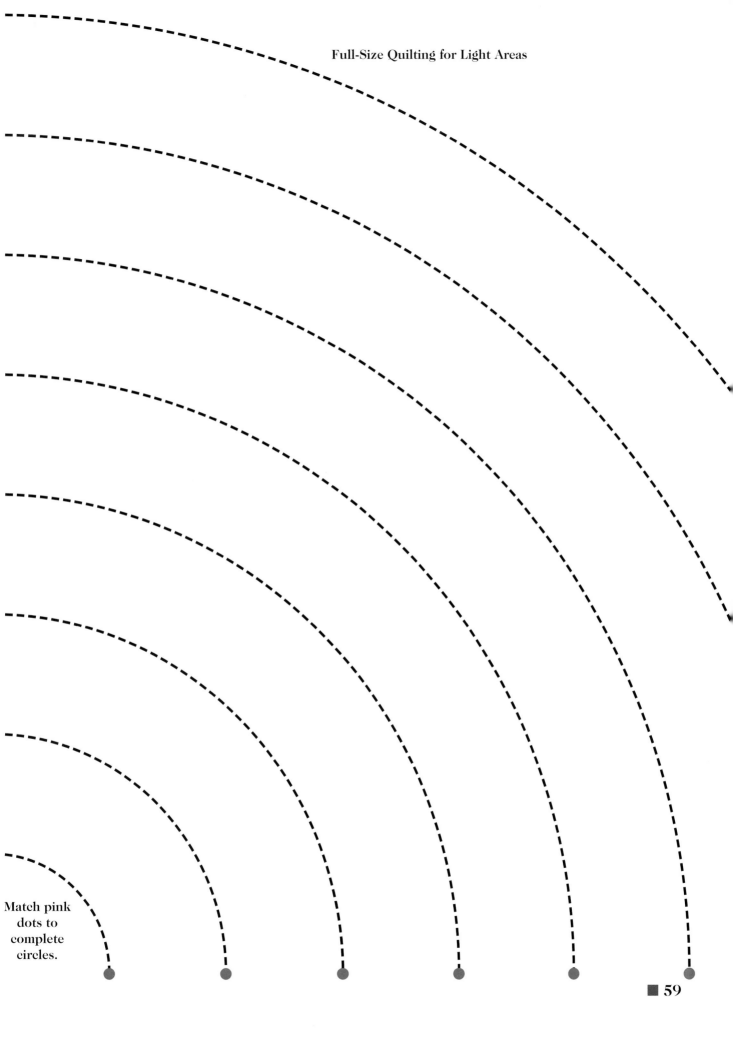

Match pink
dots to
complete
circles.

I decided on a simple, traditional Straight Furrows set for my Spring Valley Log Cabin. However, I had fun playing with the ideas below before I stitched the blocks together. The top left example has elements of Square-in-a-Square quilts and Barnraisings. At top right is a fractured Barnraising with color bands reversing shades at the midlines of the quilt. At the bottom left is a vertical strip of Sunshine and Shadows embellished with zigzags going down the two sides. At the bottom right is a Barnraising that dissolves into Sunshine and Shadows blocks in the corners of the quilt. All of the Log Cabin sets, and more, will work for Spring Valley Log Cabin. Because the log widths are uneven in light and dark halves, the line between light and dark undulates in this design. Enjoy the possibilities!

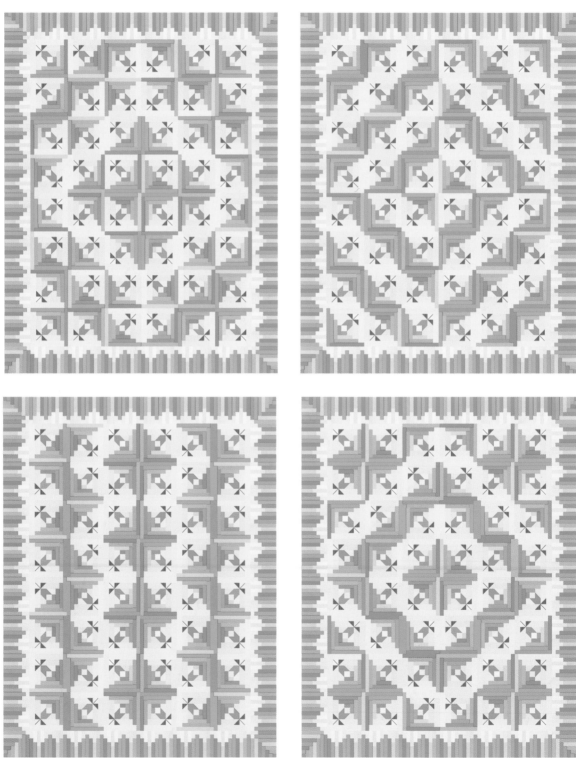

Lincoln Log Cabin

Designed and made by Judy Martin, 2002. Lincoln Log Cabin is my own variation of a traditional Log Cabin. This version has a 9-Patch superimposed on the light logs. The 9-Patch blocks reappear in the staggered border. I arranged my blocks in the all-time-favorite Barnraising set. I cut all four red or rose squares of a single 9-Patch from one fabric. I also matched dark blue logs in pairs within a block. Cutting layouts take the matched sets into account.

Made entirely from squares and rectangles, Lincoln Log Cabin is a picture of simplicity and an ideal beginner project. Any of the Log Cabin sets would be suitable for Lincoln Log Cabin. Many of the arrangements shown for other quilts in this book would be fitting for Lincoln Log Cabin, as well. On page 66, I also show some contemporary asymmetrical arrangements that might get you thinking in other directions. Have fun!

Quilt Size: 64½" x 64½" wall quilt/throw
Block Sizes: 7½" X, 4½" x 6" Y, 6" Z

Set: 6 x 6 blocks
Requires: 36 X, 44 Y, 4 Z

Yardage & Patch Quantities & Border, Binding & Lining Dimensions

Lt. Blue Background Print: 2⅜ yds.
borders (abutted):
  2 strips 2¾" x 50" (top/bottom)
  2 strips 2¾" x 45½" (sides)

408 A, 48 C, 4 D.

Dark Blue Prints: 9 fat quarters
borders (abutted):
  2 strips 2" x 65" (top/bottom)
  2 strips 2" x 62" (sides)

36 B, 36 C, 36 D, 36 E.

Yellow/Green/Pink Prints: 2 fat quarters
84 A.

Red or Rose Prints: 5 fat quarters
336 A.

Doubled Binding: ½ yd. or 2 fat quarters
  2" x 7½ yards

Lining: 4¼ yds. or 20 fat quarters
  2 panels 35" x 69"

Batting: 69" x 69"

At-a-Glance Rotary Cutting Layouts for Each Fabric

Light Blue Background Print

2-3/8 yards light blue (allows for shrinkage)

Dark Blue Prints

1 fat quarter (x 9)

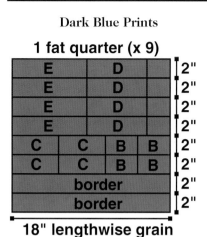

18" lengthwise grain

Yellow/Green/Pink Prints

1 fat quarter (x 2)

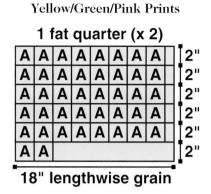

18" lengthwise grain

Red/Rose Prints

1 fat quarter (x 5)

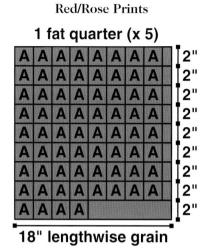

18" lengthwise grain

Binding

1 fat quarter (x 2)

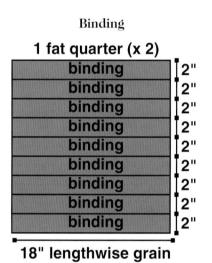

18" lengthwise grain

Lining

2 panels

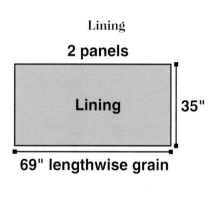

Lining — 35"

69" lengthwise grain

Details & Patch Cutting Dimensions

A. Cut 2" strip and square.

B. Cut 2" strip. Cut 3½" rectangle.

C. Cut 2" strip. Cut 5" rectangle.

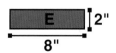

D. Cut 2" strip. Cut 6½" rectangle.

E. Cut 2" strip. Cut 8" rectangle.

Make 36 X blocks, as shown below. Also make 44 Y and 4 Z blocks for the borders. Arrange X blocks in 6 rows of 6 blocks each, playing until you arrive at an arrangement that pleases you.

Join blocks to make rows according to your layout. Join rows. Arrange Y border blocks and Z corner blocks as shown in the whole quilt diagram below.

Add shorter light blue borders to sides of quilt. Add longer light blue borders to top and bottom.

Join 11 Y's to make side borders; attach. Join 11 Y's to make top border; add a Z to each end; attach. Repeat for bottom border.

Add shorter dark blue borders to sides of quilt. Add longer dark blue borders to top and bottom.

See the quilting and finishing instructions above the quilting diagram on the next page.

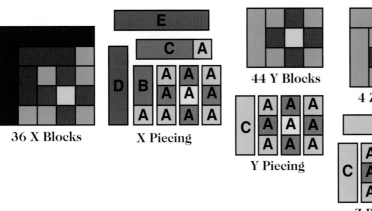

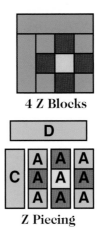

36 X Blocks **X Piecing** **44 Y Blocks** **4 Z Blocks**

Y Piecing **Z Piecing**

Note: Templates are overlapped on the page.
Patches B–E extend to the top of A.

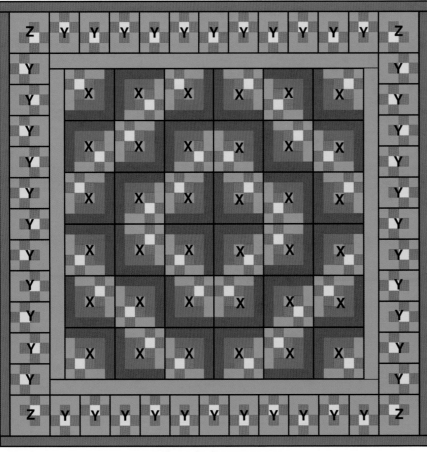

Whole Quilt Diagram

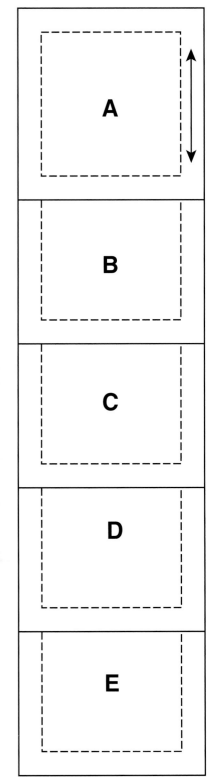

Baste the quilt top, batting, and lining together.

Quilt in the ditch around L-shaped pairs of dark blue logs. Quilt in the ditch around the red/rose nine-patch squares. Use ¾" masking tape to mark quilting lines as follows: Mark and quilt stripes ¾"

apart in the light blue. See the diagram below. Note that the stripes are perpendicular to the edges of the quilt and that the direction of the stripes changes along the quilt's diagonals.

Bind the edges. Sign and date your quilt to finish.

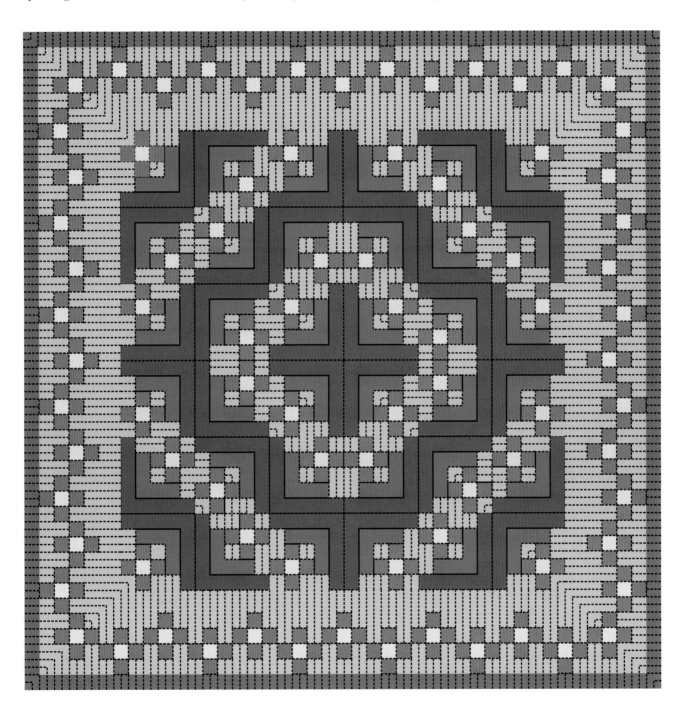

Lincoln Log Cabin is basically a Log Cabin with a 9-Patch occupying most of the light side. It plays well in traditional Log Cabin sets and in contemporary arrangements, as well. The top left example shows Lincoln Log Cabin in a traditional Straight Furrows set. At top right is a Zigzag or Streak of Lightning set. At the bottom left is a new design of reversing "X" motifs. At the bottom right is a new combination of Zigzags and Straight Furrows. I wanted to suggest woven ribbons with this design.

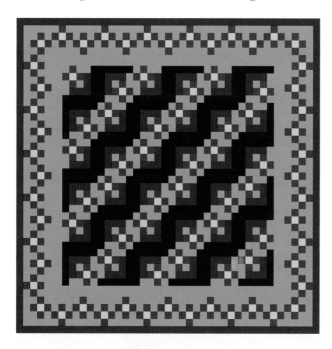

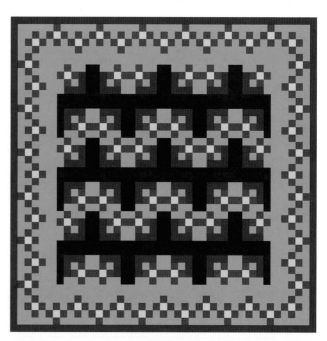

66 ∎

Thunderstruck

Designed and made by Judy Martin, 2002. The cutting and sewing are very simple. The impact comes from the brilliant colors and the lively arrangement. I chose contemporary fabrics in the clear, bright colors of citrus fruits, set off by turquoise. Light and dark values of these hues are used, with each block being half light and half dark. I used just one light fabric and one dark fabric within each block, but I used many fabrics in the quilt for a scrappy look.

The diagonal split allows this block to be set like a Log Cabin, but the zigzags change the look entirely. I like the whimsical asymmetry of this irregular arrangement. Although I made the blocks with no thought as to their arrangement, I found myself stringing together similarly-colored blocks for continuity. You may prefer a more random approach. Have fun playing not only with the light-dark pattern but also with the color placement details.

Quilt Size: 51" x 63¾" wall quilt/throw
Block Size: 6" Y, 2⅛" Z

Set: 6 x 8 blocks
Requires: 48 Y blocks, 92 Z border units

Light Prints: 12 fat quarters
borders (abutted):
  2 strips 4⅛" x 43" (top/bottom)
  2 strips 3¾" x 48½" (sides)

236 A, 48 B, 48 C, 4 D.

Bright Prints: 12 fat quarters
borders (abutted):
  2 strips 2⅝" x 51½" (top/bottom)

2 strips 2⅝" x 60" (sides)

236 A, 48 B, 48 C.

Doubled Binding: ½ yd. or 2 fat quarters
  2" x 6¾ yards

Lining: 4⅛ yds. or 15 fat quarters
  2 panels 28" x 68"

Batting: 55" x 68"

At-a-Glance Rotary Cutting Layouts for Each Fabric

Light Prints

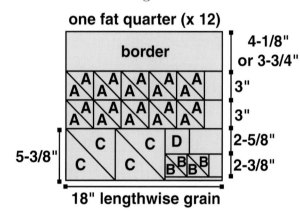

Bright Prints

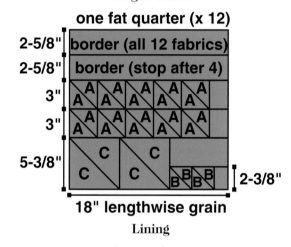

Binding

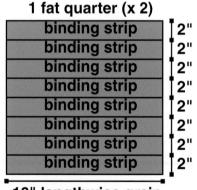

Lining

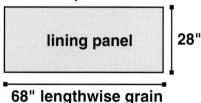

Details & Patch Cutting Dimensions for Cutting Layouts

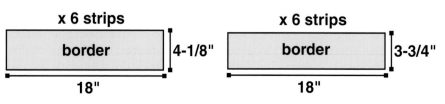

Each fat quarter yields enough patches for the light or dark half of 4 blocks as well as pieced and plain borders.

Light Borders: Cut 6 strips 4⅛" x 18" and 6 strips 3¾" x 18".

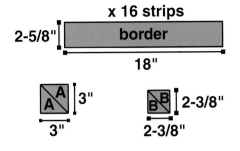

x 16 strips

2-5/8" | border |

18"

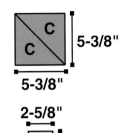

A | 3"

3"

B | 2-3/8"

2-3/8"

C | 5-3/8"

5-3/8"

2-5/8"

D | 2-5/8"

Bright Borders: Cut 16 strips 2⅝" x 18". That is, cut 2 border strips from each of the first 4 fat quarters. Cut 1 border strip from each fat quarter thereafter.

A: Cut 3" strips and squares. Cut each square in half along one diagonal to make 2 triangles. Trim points.

B: Cut 2⅜" strips and squares. Cut each square in half along one diagonal to make 2 triangles. Trim points.

C: Cut 5⅜" strips and squares. Cut each square in half along one diagonal to make 2 triangles. Trim points.

D: Cut 2⅝" strips and squares.

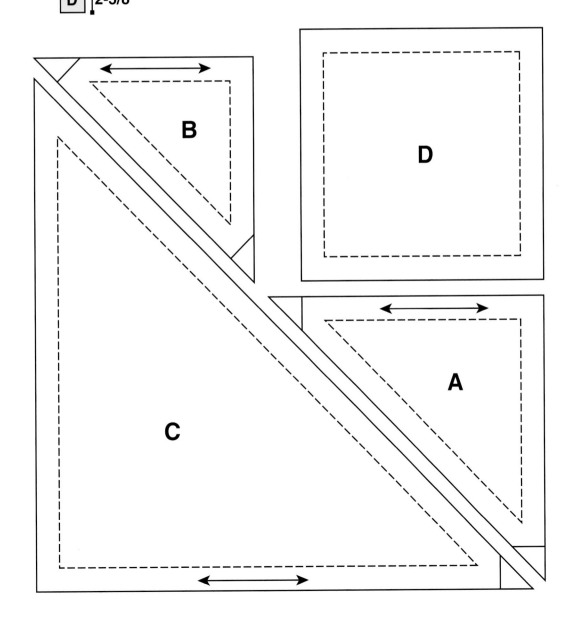

Make 48 Y blocks for the quilt center and 92 Z units for the pieced borders. Play with the Y block arrangement, placing blocks in 8 rows of 6 blocks each. When you have decided on a favorite arrangement, join blocks to make rows. Join rows.

Attach the narrower light border strips to the sides of the quilt center. Add wider light strips to top and bottom of quilt center.

To make the pieced border for the long side of the quilt, join 13 Z units facing the same direction. Join 13 more facing the opposite direction. Sew together to make one long strip, with light triangles touching at the center. Pin and stitch to the side of the quilt. Repeat for the opposite side. To make the top border, join 10 Z's facing one way and 10 Z's facing the opposite way. Sew a light D to each end. Sew to the top of the quilt. Repeat for the bottom of the quilt.

Attach the longer dark border strips to the sides of the quilt center. Add the shorter dark strips to the top and bottom of the quilt center.

To finish the quilt, refer to the quilting directions above the quilting diagram on page 71.

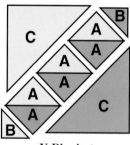

48 Y Blocks

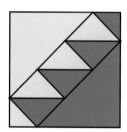

Y Piecing

92 Z Border Units

Z Piecing

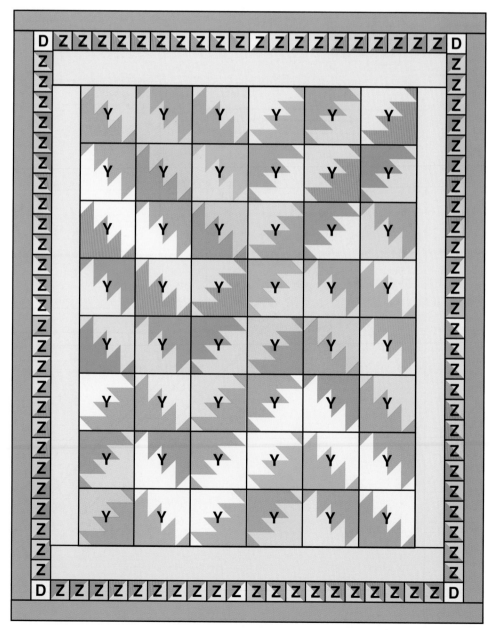

Whole Quilt Diagram

Mark the quarter-circle quilting from page 72 in the light triangles and light borders as shown below.

Baste the layers together. Quilt as marked.

Quilt in the ditch between dark and light patches of the Y blocks. Use ¼" masking tape to mark and quilt a row of echo quilting on the dark halves of the Y blocks ¼" in from the quilting in the ditch. Similarly mark and quilt another line of echo quilting ¼" farther in. Quilt in the ditch along both sides of the light inner border.

Quilt in the ditch along the short sides of pieced border triangles. Also quilt in the ditch along the long sides of these triangles, extending the lines through the dark outer border. Use ¾" masking tape to mark parallel quilting lines halfway between these. Quilt "V" shapes in the center of each dark outer border, as shown. Quilt diagonal lines in each corner of the quilt, extending across the D squares and the outer border corners.

Bind, sign and date the quilt to complete it.

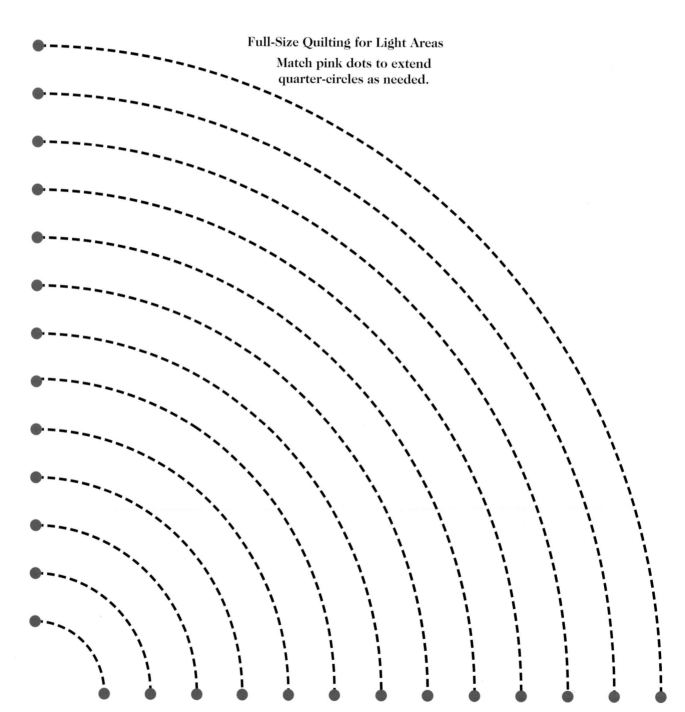

Full-Size Quilting for Light Areas
Match pink dots to extend
quarter-circles as needed.

The top left example combines a Zigzag with a Sunshine and Shadows arrangement. At top right is a quilt arranged to make concentric "X" motifs. At the bottom left is an asymmetrical spiral. At bottom right is a set of five small Barnraisings split at the midlines to reverse colors. The first three blend colors of neighboring blocks. The final example uses blending in some areas and contrast in others.

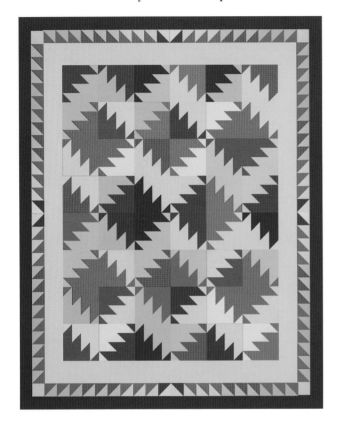 

Family Farm

Designed and pieced by Judy Martin; quilted by Jean Nolte, 2002. The blocks for Family Farm were shown on my web site in a variety of arrangements. Readers voted for their preferred sets, and this is the one that won. The blocks make four-pointed stars alternating with hour glasses here. Some shapes are unusual, but they can be readily rotary cut. Even the paper cut-away template is rotary cut, so you won't lose any of your cutting momentum.

I used just two fabrics for the four patches of each block. The cutting layouts allow for matching the scraps within a block. The sewing is exceptionally easy. Fabrics include some from Moda and Marcus Brothers. Batting is 100% cotton from Hobbs.

Quilt Size: 84" x 96" twin/double
Block Size: 6"

Set: 12 x 14 blocks
Requires: 84 X, 84 Y, R16 ruler (optional)

Yardage & Patch Quantities & Border, Binding & Lining Dimensions

Dark Prints: 35 fat quarters
borders (abutted):
  2 strips 4½" x 96½" (sides)
  2 strips 4½" x 76½" (top/bottom)

84 A, 84 B, 84 Br, 84 C, 26 D, 2 E.

Light Prints: 27 fat quarters
84 A, 84 B, 84 Br, 84 C, 26 D, 2 E.

Doubled Binding: ¾ yd. or **3 fat quarters**
  2" x 10½ yards

Lining: 7⅛ yds. or **35 fat quarters**
  3 panels 34" x 88"

Batting: 88" x 100"

At-a-Glance Rotary Cutting Layouts for Each Fabric

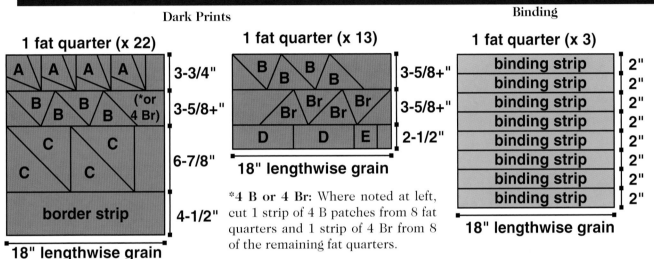

Dark Prints

1 fat quarter (x 22)
A A A A — 3-3/4"
B B B B (*or 4 Br) — 3-5/8+"
C C C C — 6-7/8"
border strip — 4-1/2"
18" lengthwise grain

1 fat quarter (x 13)
B B B — 3-5/8+"
Br Br Br — 3-5/8+"
D D E — 2-1/2"
18" lengthwise grain

*4 B or 4 Br: Where noted at left, cut 1 strip of 4 B patches from 8 fat quarters and 1 strip of 4 Br from 8 of the remaining fat quarters.

Binding

1 fat quarter (x 3)
binding strip — 2"
binding strip — 2"
binding strip — 2"
binding strip — 2"
binding strip — 2"
binding strip — 2"
binding strip — 2"
binding strip — 2"
18" lengthwise grain

Light Prints

1 fat quarter (x 21)
A A A A — 3-3/4"
B B B B (*or 4 Br) — 3-5/8+"
C C C C — 6-7/8"
D — 2-1/2"
18" lengthwise grain

1 fat quarter (x 6)
B B B — 3-5/8+"
B B B — 3-5/8+"
Br Br Br — 3-5/8+"
Br Br Br — 3-5/8+"
D E — 2-1/2"
18" lengthwise grain

Lining

x 3 panels
lining — 34"
88" lengthwise grain

Details & Patch Cutting Dimensions for Cutting Layouts

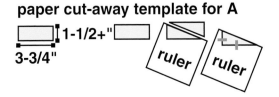

paper cut-away template for A
3-3/4" — 1-1/2+"
ruler / ruler

A. Start by making a paper cut-away template. From a piece of plain white paper, rotary cut a strip 1½+" wide (halfway between 1½" and 1⅝"). From this strip, cut a rectangle 3¾" long. Cut this in half along one diagonal, as shown at left, to make 2 triangles. Tape one triangle to a rotary ruler with the long edge of the paper triangle along the edge of the ruler.

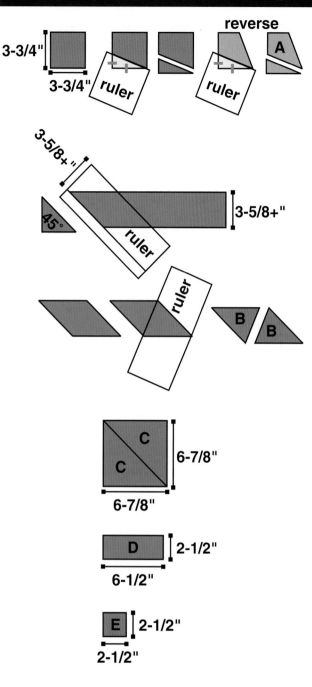

A (continued). Cut a fabric strip 3¾" wide. Cut a 3¾" square. Lay the cut-away template over the fabric square, with the two shorter sides of the template aligned with two sides of the square. Cut along the edge of the ruler. Turn the resulting shape face down. Align the cutting template over the shape as shown. Cut along the edge of the ruler to complete A, a kite shape.

B. Note: Half of the B strips should be subcut face down to make Br. The only difference between B and Br is the grainline. Cut mirror images to keep straight grain around the edges of the blocks.

Cut a strip 3⅝+" wide, using my Rotaruler 16 or using a regular rotary ruler and "eyeballing" halfway between the 3⅝" line and the 3¾" line. Cut off one end at a 45° angle.

Lay the 3⅝+" line of the Rotaruler 16 (or eyeball, as described above) even with the angled end of the strip. Cut along the edge of the ruler to complete a diamond. Place the edge of the ruler from corner to corner of the diamond, as shown. Cut in half to complete 2 B triangles.

C. Cut a strip 6⅞" wide. Cut a 6⅞" square. Cut in half along one diagonal to make 2 C triangles.

D. Cut a strip 2½" wide. Cut a 6½" rectangle.

E. Cut a strip 2½" wide. Cut a 2½" square.

Construction

Make 84 X blocks and 84 Y blocks as shown on page 77. Play with sets, placing blocks in 14 rows of 12 blocks each. Join blocks to make rows. Join rows.

For the pieced borders, join 7 dark D rectangles alternately with 7 light D's. Sew to the long edge of the quilt. (In my set, dark D's touch light C's of the blocks. Your set may vary.) Repeat for the opposite side. Join 6 dark D's alternately with 6 light D's. Sew

a dark E square to the light end and a light E to the dark end. Sew to the top of quilt. Repeat for the bottom of the quilt.

Attach the shorter plain border strips to the top and bottom of the quilt. Add longer plain strips to the sides of the quilt.

Quilting and finishing are described above the quilting diagram on page 78.

84 X Blocks

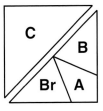

84 Y Blocks

X & Y Piecing

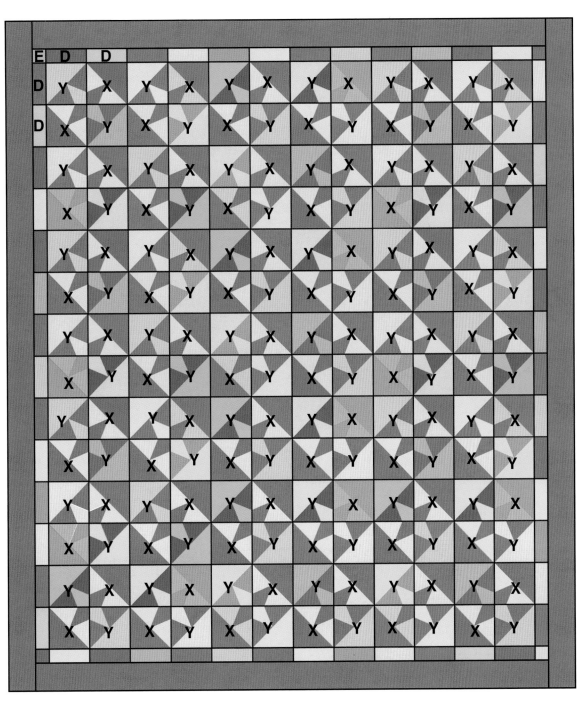

Whole Quilt Diagram

Mark the flower motif on the large C triangles, completing the motifs around the edges by extending them into the borders.

Baste the layers together. Quilt as marked.

Quilt in the ditch around the kite shapes (A's). Quilt in the ditch between block halves, again continuing these lines into the border. Use masking tape to mark another line 1" from this line, but not crossing the A patches. Quilt along the edge of the masking tape. Also use masking tape to mark a line 1" in from the outer edge of the quilt, not crossing the previous lines of quilting. Quilt along the edge of the tape.

Bind the quilt. Sign and date it to finish.

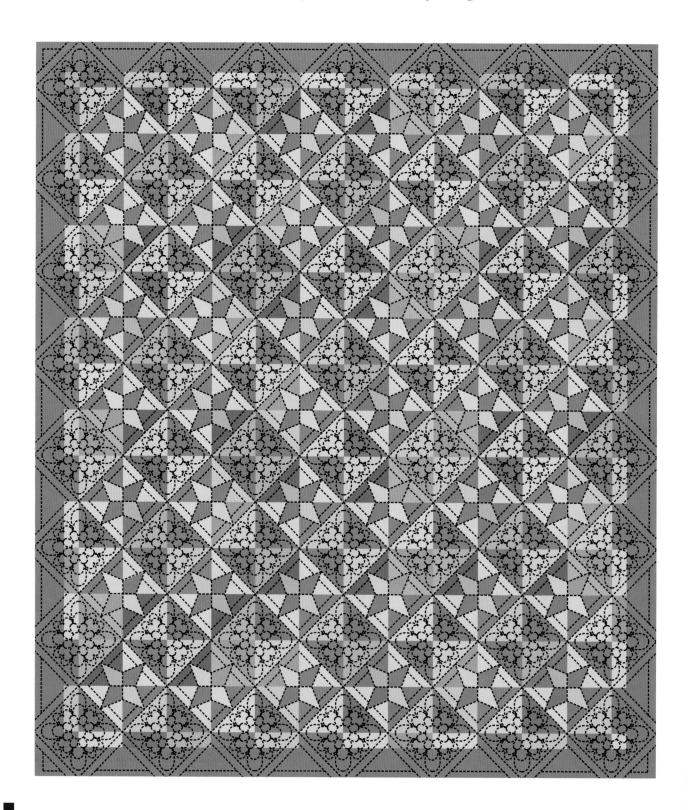

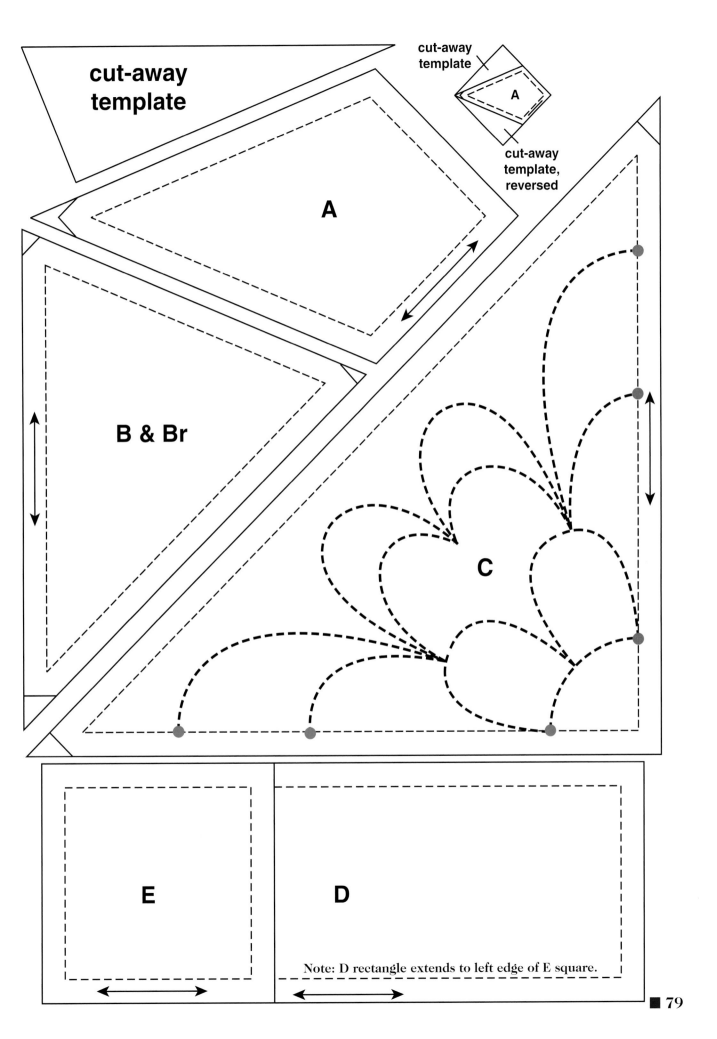

cut-away template

cut-away template

A

cut-away template, reversed

A

B & Br

C

E

D

Note: D rectangle extends to left edge of E square.

■ 79

I like to think of Family Farm as a "half-prickly Log Cabin." The half block composed of one large triangle yields a smoother line than the typical Log Cabin. The side composed of a kite and two small triangles makes a spiked edge that is less smooth than a Log Cabin. The juxtaposition of smooth and spikey adds an interesting twist. The top left example is an irregularly spaced Zigzag. At top right is a pattern of many small, reversing Barnraisings. At the bottom left is a combination of Sunshine and Shadows and Zigzag. At the bottom right, the blocks are arranged to form Zigzags. However, smooth and prickly Zigzags result from this particular block for a look that resembles a Delectable Mountains pattern.

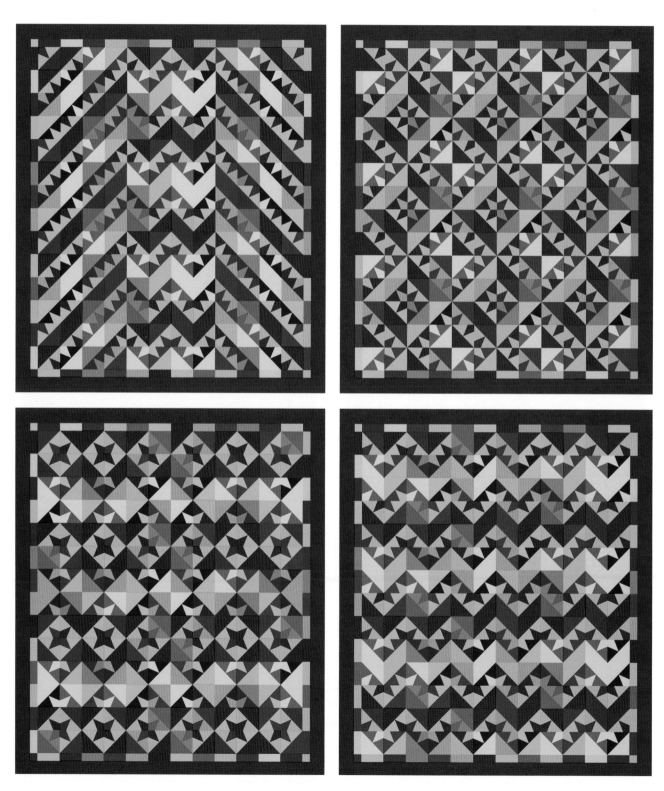

Steve's Star

Designed by Steve Bennett; pieced by Judy Martin; quilted by Jean Nolte, 2002. This was Steve's first attempt at designing. What can I say? I must be a genius to have married him.

I love this quilt! Both types of blocks are split diagonally into light and dark halves. All the Log Cabin sets (and more!) are play options. The more I play with the blocks, the more I want to play with them. I can see myself making this quilt over and over again.

The quilt is easy to sew, but the shapes of the star block do not lend themselves to rotary cutting. I made the quilt using paper templates taped to a rotary ruler. I provide templates for you to use as I did or to use traditionally. I heartily recommend that you trim points as shown on the templates in order to help you align the patches for stitching.

For those of you who prefer paper piecing, I also offer a paper foundation pattern.

Quilt Size: 48" x 60" wall quilt or throw
Block Size: 6"

Set: 6 x 8 blocks
Requires: 28 Y, 24 Z

Yardage & Patch Quantities & Border, Binding & Lining Dimensions

Cream Prints: 10 fat quarters
28 Ar, 28 B, 28 C, 28 D, 28 E, 24 F.

Red Prints: 5 fat quarters
28 A, 28 C, 24 F.

Navy Blue Prints: 4 fat quarters
28 Br, 28 Dr, 28 Er.

Navy Borders: 1½ yds. or 4 fat quarters
borders (abutted):

2 strips 6½" x 36½" (top/bottom)
2 strips 6½" x 48½" (sides)

Doubled Binding: ½ yd. or 2 fat quarters
2" x 6½ yards

Lining: 3⅛ yds. or 12 fat quarters
2 panels 33" x 52"

Batting: 52" x 64"

Cutting Instructions

cream prints
For 24 F, rotary cut 6 strips 6⅞" x 18". Subcut two 6⅞" squares from each strip. Cut each square in half along one diagonal to make 2 triangles. Trim points.

Cut remaining cream patches using templates or use scraps to fit the paper piecing foundations.

red prints
For 24 F, rotary cut 6 strips 6⅞" x 18". Subcut two 6⅞" squares from each strip. Cut each square in half along one diagonal to make 2 triangles. Trim points.

Cut remaining red patches using templates or use scraps for paper piecing.

navy blue prints
Cut navy blue patches using templates or use scraps to fit the paper foundations.

navy blue print for border
Cut 2 borders 6½" x 36½" (top/bottom).
Cut 2 borders 6½" x 48½" (sides).

doubled binding
Rotary cut 14 strips 2" x 18".

lining
Rotary cut 2 panels 33" x 52".

Construction

The Y blocks (stars) can be made with traditional cutting and piecing methods, using the templates on page 85. They can also be made using paper foundation piecing as described on page 86.

Make 28 Y blocks and 24 Z blocks as shown on page 83. Set aside 4 Y blocks for the border corners. Play with block arrangements, using the diagram on page 83 and drawings on page 87 to get you started.

Join blocks in 8 rows of 6 blocks each. Join rows.

Add longer navy borders to sides of quilt. Sew a Y block to both ends of each shorter border, turning these star blocks so that the blue is in the outer corners, as shown in the quilt diagram on page 83. Sew to top and bottom of quilt. Tear away the paper foundations if you used them.

Finish the quilt as described on page 84.

28 Y Blocks

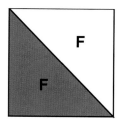

Y Piecing

Br Er
B
Ar C
A Dr
E C
D

24 Z Blocks

Z Piecing

F
F

Whole Quilt Diagram

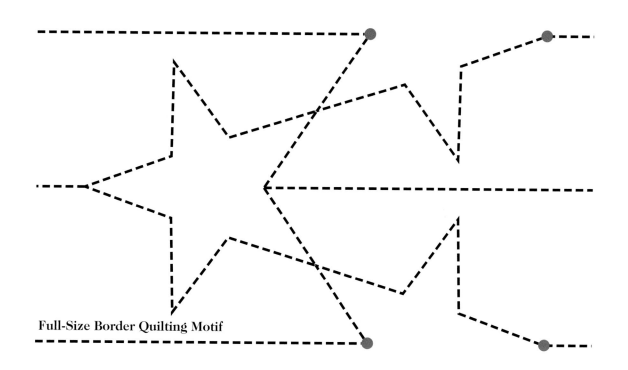

Full-Size Border Quilting Motif

Mark the star motif from page 83 in the navy borders. (You can use masking tape to mark the background stripes later, if you like.) Mark additional stars from the F patch on page 85 to fill the cream areas as shown.

Baste the layers together.

In the red areas, use masking tape to mark radiating lines from the corners of the quilt (excluding borders). Also use masking tape to mark radiating lines from the center of the quilt as shown. Use masking tape to mark quilting lines ½" from the edges of the cream areas, 1" and 2" from the edges of the center blue area. If you haven't already marked them, use masking tape to mark background stripes in borders as shown in border quilting motif on page 83.

Quilt as marked. Quilt in the ditch around stars and along the diagonals of all blocks.

Bind the edges. Sign and date your quilt to finish.

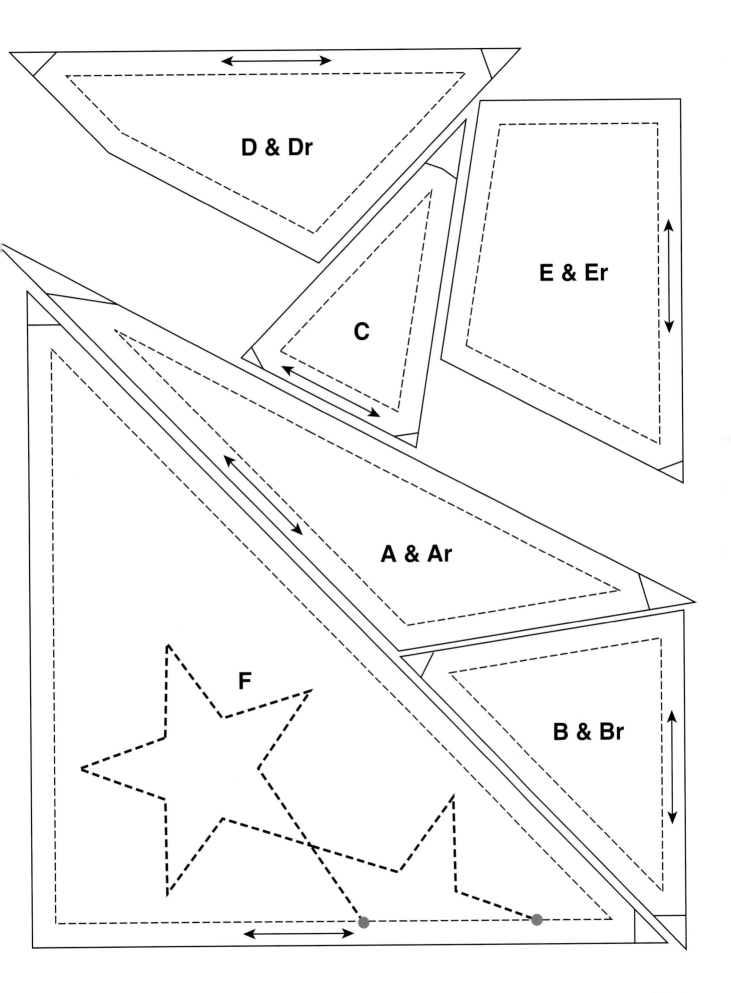

D & Dr

E & Er

C

A & Ar

F

B & Br

Cut the patches oversized for paper foundation piecing, and trim down after attaching.

Make 28 accurately sized photocopies or tracings of this page. The star block is made in two sections. Pin patches to the back of the paper, and stitch on the lines from the front. For section I, lay a cream patch to cover the area marked "#1" on the paper foundation. Lay a blue patch over the area marked "#2," then flip it over #1 so that right sides are together, and stitch on the line, using a small machine stitch. Flip the blue patch back to make

sure it covers #2. Trim the patches down to ¼" outside the seam lines of the foundation. Continue adding patches in numerical order through #5 for section I. Trim fabric even with cutting lines at edge of paper foundation.

Make section II similarly, adding patches #6–#10 in numerical order. Sew the two sections together. It is important to leave the paper foundations attached to stabilize the blocks. After completing the quilt top, stay stitch the edges of the 4 corner blocks, and tear away the paper foundations.

paper foundation section I

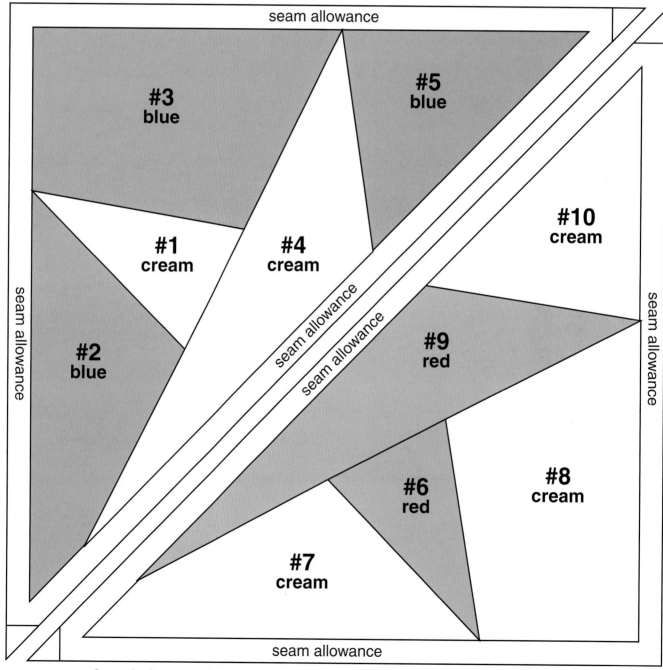

paper foundation section II

In the top left example, a Pinwheel is framed with triangles and a ring of stars. The corners form a Barnraising pattern. At top right is an arrangement of red stars edged on two sides with scallops made from smaller stars. Zigzags prevail in the bottom left example. At bottom right, chevrons make a strong pattern. The placement of light and dark forms only part of the pattern in this quilt. The placement of small stars plays a role in defining the various arrangements, as well.

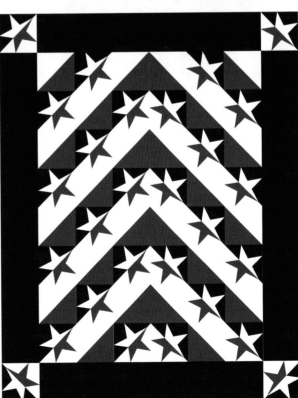

America, the Beautiful

Designed by Will Bennett; pieced by Judy Martin; quilted by Jean Nolte, 2002. My 10-year-old son designed the America, the Beautiful block. It is not his first design effort, but I think it is his best one yet. (I had better watch out or my whole family will eclipse me as pattern designers!)

This design is not so much a pattern of light and dark as a graphic statement in stars and stripes. Blocks having red edges alternate with blocks having white edges to create many exciting setting possibilities. I matched fabrics in stars and log pairs within a block. Cutting layouts allow for this matching.

Quilt Size: 76½" x 97½" twin/double
Block Size: 10½" V, W; 12" X; 10½" x 12" Y, Z

Set: 5 x 7 blocks
Requires: 18 V, 17 W, 4 X, 14 Y, 10 Z, S45 tool

Yardage & Patch Quantities & Binding & Lining Dimensions

Cream Prints: 20 fat quarters
39 A, 312 C, 22 E, 39 F, 39 G, 94 H.

Red Prints: 19 fat quarters
17 E, 39 F, 39 G, 93 H, 4 I.

Navy Blue Prints: 10 fat quarters
156 B, 156 D, 24 J.

Doubled Binding: ¾ yd. or 3 fat quarters
2" x 10 yards

Lining: 7¼ yds. or 35 fat quarters
3 panels 35" x 81"

Batting:
81" x 102"

At-a-Glance Rotary Cutting Layouts for Each Fabric

Cream Prints

one fat quarter (x 20)

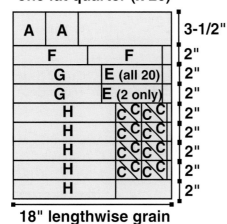

Navy Blue Prints

1 fat quarter (x 10)

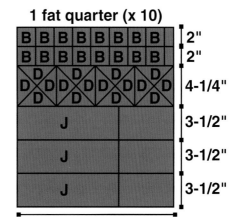

Red Prints

one fat quarter (x 16)   **one fat quarter (x 3)**

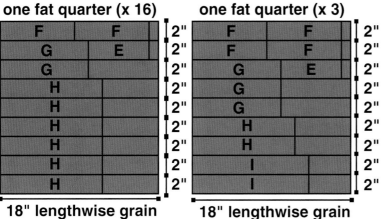

Binding

1 fat quarter (x 3)

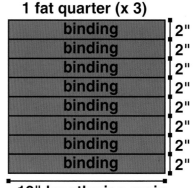

Lining

x 3 panels

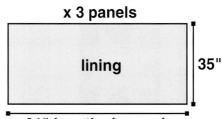

A. Cut 3½" strip and square.

 **D.** Cut 4¼" strip and square. Cut in half along both diagonals to complete 4 D triangles.

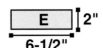 **B.** Cut 2" strip and square.

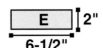 **E.** Cut 2" strip. Cut 6½" rectangle.

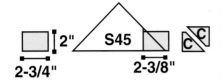 **C. Note** that the C triangle is the same finished patch as a half-square triangle.

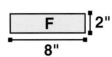 **F.** Cut 2" strip. Cut 8" rectangle.

However, this C is cut from the narrower strip needed for the other patches. Therefore, this C is cut 2 to a rectangle, and the rectangle is not cut along its diagonal, but using the S45 tool.

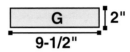 **G.** Cut 2" strip. Cut 9½" rectangle.

Cut 2" strip. Cut 2¾" rectangle. Subcut each rectangle to make 2 triangles using the Shapemaker 45 tool as follows: Align the 2⅜" line of the S45 tool with short end of rectangle. (The point of the tool is about ⅜" from the right corner.) Align long edge of S45 even with long side of rectangle. Cut along the angled end of the tool to make two triangles, each with one point pretrimmed. Trim remaining point of each triangle.

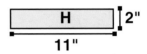 **H.** Cut 2" strip. Cut 11" rectangle.

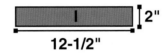 **I.** Cut 2" strip. Cut 12½" rectangle.

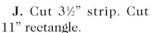 **J.** Cut 3½" strip. Cut 11" rectangle.

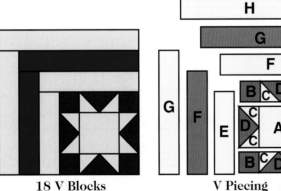

18 V Blocks   **V Piecing**

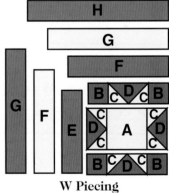

17 W Blocks   **W Piecing**

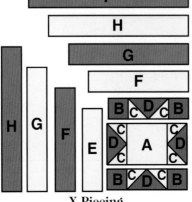

4 X Blocks   **X Piecing**

Make 18 V blocks, 17 W blocks, 4 X blocks, 14 Y blocks, and 10 Z blocks, as shown on page 90 and below. Arrange V and W blocks in 7 rows of 5 blocks each. Piece 'n' Play to arrive at your favorite setting. Join blocks to make rows. Join rows.

Referring to the whole quilt diagram below, join 4 Y blocks alternately with 3 Z. Sew to the side of the quilt. Repeat for the other side. Join 3 Y blocks alternately with 2 Z. Sew an X to each end. Sew to the top of the quilt. Repeat for the bottom.

To finish the quilt, see the quilting instructions above the quilting diagram on page 92.

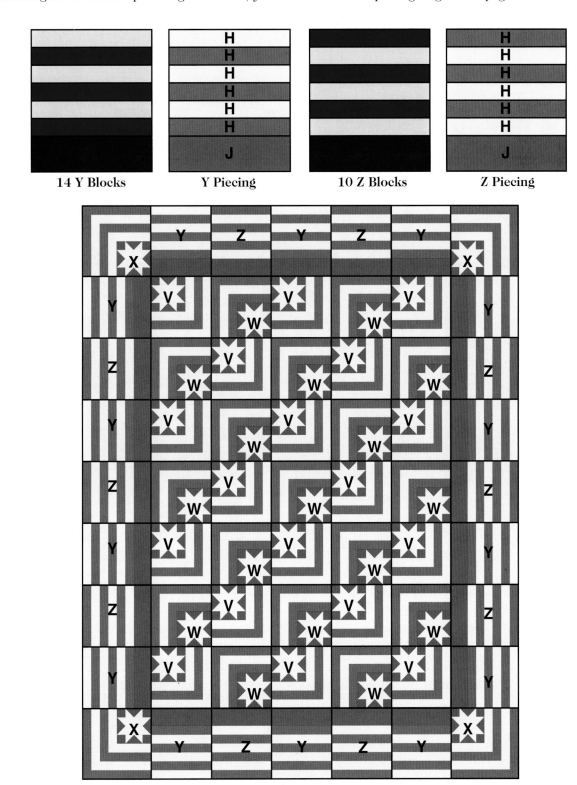

14 Y Blocks   Y Piecing   10 Z Blocks   Z Piecing

Whole Quilt Diagram

Mark the starburst motif from page 94 in each cream star. (You need not mark in the ditch.)

Baste the layers together. Quilt as marked.

Quilt in the ditch around the blue B and D patches that form the background of the stars.

Use masking tape to mark straight-line quilting in red and cream rectangles of blocks as follows:

Parallel stripes go from corner to corner of red and cream rectangles of Y and Z blocks in borders. In V, W, and X blocks, stripes go in parallel V's as shown. Also mark stripes 1½" apart in blue J rectangles of borders. Quilt as marked.

Bind the quilt's edges. Sign and date your quilt to finish it.

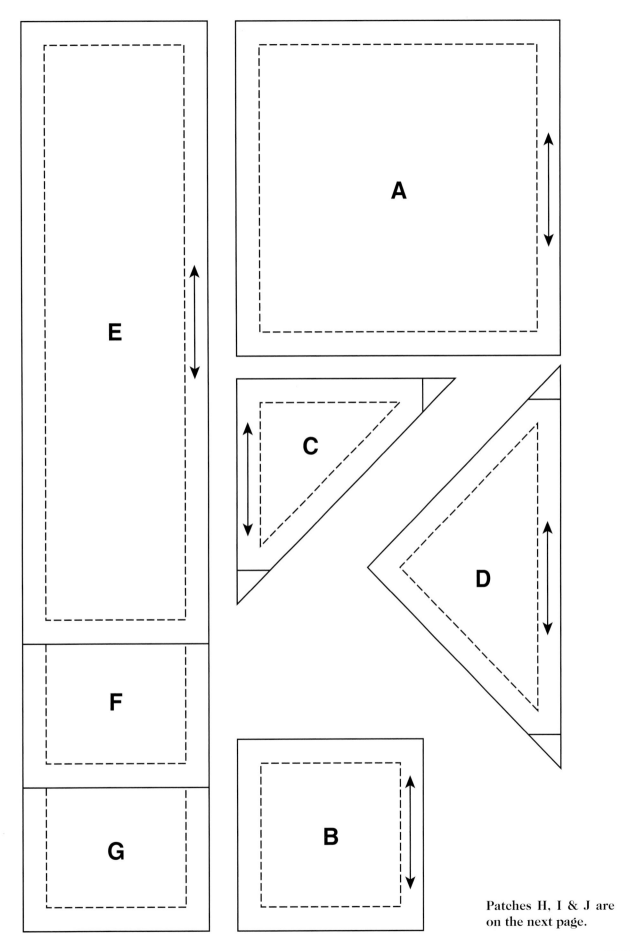

Patches H, I & J are
on the next page.

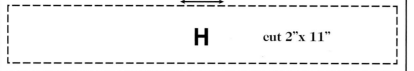

H   cut 2"x 11"

H, I & J at left are shown smaller than their actual sizes because they are too large to fit the page. Cut patches the listed sizes.

I   cut 2"x 12½"

J   cut 3½"x 11"

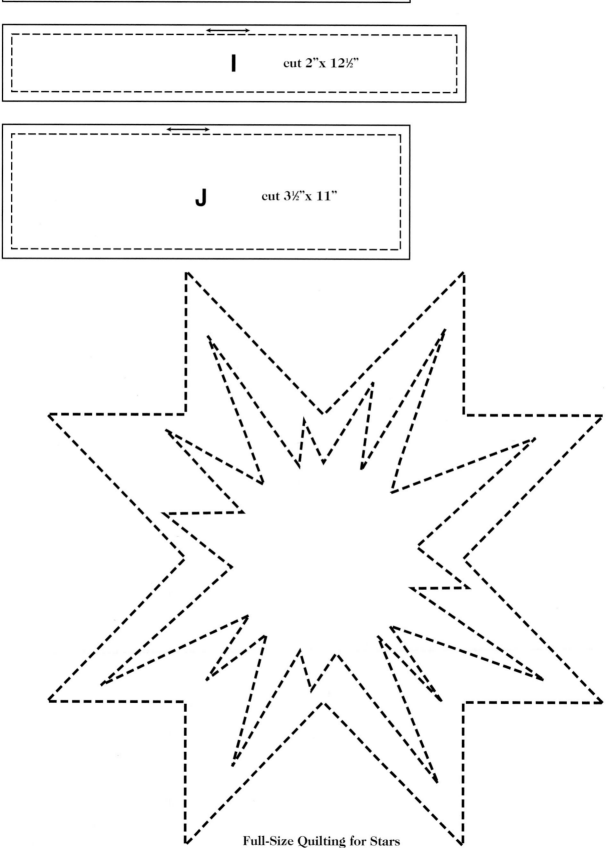

Full-Size Quilting for Stars

This pair of blocks plays a little differently because it is not simply divided into light and dark halves. Stripes make a strong statement here. Framed boxes, half-framed boxes and stair-stepped chains are a few of the possibilities. Additional possibilities result from clustering matching or contrasting blocks.

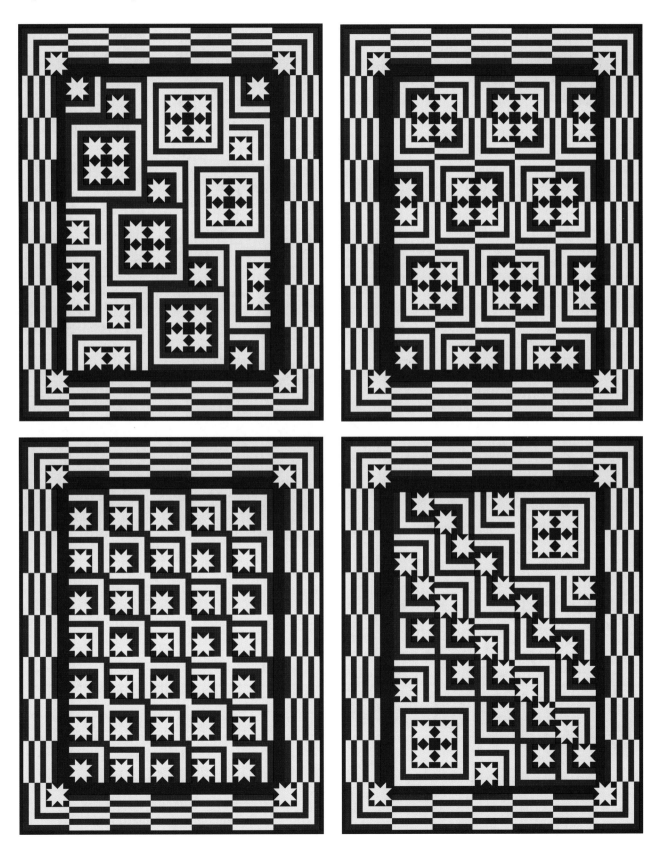

Judy Martin made her first quilt as a college student. She made patchwork comforters for sale and taught quiltmaking in the early '70s. In 1979, she joined the staff of *Quilter's Newsletter Magazine* as an editor. Her job entailed designing quilts and writing patterns for both *QNM* and *Quiltmaker* magazines. While there, she also wrote six books, including *Scrap Quilts*.

Eight years later, Judy left the magazines to write books at home and start a family. In 1988, she and her husband, Steve Bennett, working together as Crosley-Griffith Publishing Company, Inc., produced their first self-published book, *Judy Martin's Ultimate Book of Quilt Block Patterns*. Ten books and two children later, Judy and Steve continue to make their living with Crosley-Griffith Publishing Company, Inc.

In addition to her books, Judy has designed three rotary cutting tools to help quilters accurately cut patches in a wide variety of shapes and sizes.

Through her books and tools, Judy aims to provide quilters with the skills and confidence they need to make any quilt that they can imagine.

Judy has enough original quilt designs in her files to keep her busy making quilts and writing books for years. She enjoys reading, tandem bicycling, playing word games, and collecting fabric, quilt tops, and bunnies.

Find out more about Judy and her books and quilts on her web site:

www.judymartin.com

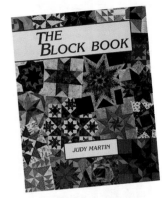

Shakespeare in the Park from The Creative Pattern Book *and "I Have a Dream" from* Cookies 'n' Quilts *are just two of the hundreds of original quilt patterns Judy Martin has published.*

Books

Cookies 'n' Quilts, Star Happy Quilts, The Creative Pattern Book, The Block Book, Judy Martin's Ultimate Rotary Cutting Reference, and *Pieced Borders* coauthored with Marsha McCloskey.

Tools

Point Trimmer, Shapemaker 45, and Rotaruler 16.

Available from:

CROSLEY-GRIFFITH
PUBLISHING COMPANY, INC.
P.O. Box 512
Grinnell, IA 50112
(800) 642-5615 in U.S.A.
(641) 236-4854 phone or fax
email: info@judymartin.com
web site: www.judymartin.com